What Readers Are Saying About
HTML5 and CSS3

This book does an excellent job of cutting through the hype and telling you what you need to know to navigate the HTML5 waters.

➤ **Casey Helbling**
Founder, Clear :: Software for Good

If you are looking to take advantage of the emerging HTML5 standard, then this is your book. Brian's practical experience and examples show you how to develop robust web applications amid all the support differences of today's browsers.

➤ **Mark Nichols**
Microsoft Senior consultant and cohost, DeveloperSmackdown.com Podcast

Learning HTML5 and CSS3 has improved my ability to work on cutting-edge projects. I just started a project using HTML5, and I would not have felt confident without this book.

➤ **Noel Rappin**
    Senior consultant, Obtiva, and author, *Rails Test Prescriptions*

Brian's book effortlessly guides you through crafting a site in HTML5 and CSS3 that works in all browsers; it describes what works now, what doesn't, and what to watch out for as the standards and browsers evolve.

➤ **Doug Rhoten**
    Senior software developer, InterFlow

HTML5 and CSS3

Develop with Tomorrow's Standards Today

Brian P. Hogan

The Pragmatic Bookshelf

Dallas, Texas • Raleigh, North Carolina

Many of the designations used by manufacturers and sellers to distinguish their products are claimed as trademarks. Where those designations appear in this book, and The Pragmatic Programmers, LLC was aware of a trademark claim, the designations have been printed in initial capital letters or in all capitals. The Pragmatic Starter Kit, The Pragmatic Programmer, Pragmatic Programming, Pragmatic Bookshelf, PragProg and the linking *g* device are trademarks of The Pragmatic Programmers, LLC.

Every precaution was taken in the preparation of this book. However, the publisher assumes no responsibility for errors or omissions, or for damages that may result from the use of information (including program listings) contained herein.

Our Pragmatic courses, workshops, and other products can help you and your team create better software and have more fun. For more information, as well as the latest Pragmatic titles, please visit us at *http://pragprog.com*.

The team that produced this book includes:

Susannah Pfalzer (editor)
Potomac Indexing, LLC (indexer)
Kim Wimpsett (copyeditor)
David J Kelly (typesetter)
Janet Furlow (producer)
Juliet Benda (rights)
Ellie Callahan (support)

Printed in the United States of America.
ISBN-13: 978-1-934356-68-5
Printed on acid-free paper.
Book version: P4.0—December 2011

Contents

Part II — New Sights and Sounds

Part III — Beyond HTML5

Acknowledgments

I jumped into writing this book before I had even finished my previous one, and although most of my friends, family, and probably the publisher thought I was crazy for not taking a bit of a break, they have all been so supportive. This book is a result of so many wonderful and helpful people.

First, I can't thank Dave Thomas and Andy Hunt enough for giving me the opportunity to work with them a second time. Their feedback throughout this process has helped shape this book quite a bit, and I'm honored to be a Pragmatic Bookshelf author.

Daniel Steinberg helped me get this book started, signed, and on the right track early on, and I'm very grateful for all the support he gave and the things he taught me about how to write clearly. Whenever I write, I still hear his voice guiding me in the right direction.

Daniel was unable to continue working with me on this book, but he left me in unbelievably good hands. Susannah Pfalzer has been so amazingly helpful throughout this entire process, keeping me on track, pushing me to do better, and always knowing exactly the right questions to ask me at exactly the right times. Without Susannah, this book wouldn't be nearly as good.

My technical reviewers for both rounds were extremely helpful in shaping a lot of the content and its presentation. Thank you, Aaron Godin, Ali Raza, Charles Leffingwell, Daniel Steinberg, David Kulberg, Don Henton, Doug Rhoten, Edi Schlechtinger, Jon Mischo, Jon Oebser, Kevin Gisi, Marc Harter, Mark Nichols, Noel Rappin, Paul Neibarger, Sam Elliott, Sean Canton, Srdjan Pejic, Stephen Wolff, Todd Dahl, and Erik Watson.

Special thanks to the fine folks at ZenCoder for assisting with the video encoding for the sample files and for making it much easier for content producers to prepare video for HTML5.

Thank you to my business associates Chris Johnson, Chris Warren, Mike Weber, Jon Kinney, Adam Ludwig, Gary Crabtree, Carl Hoover, Josh Anderson,

Austen Ott, and Nick Lamuro for the support on this and many other projects. Special thanks to Erich Tesky for the reality checks and for being a great friend when things got frustrating.

I also want to thank my dad for always expecting me to do my best and for pushing me to not give up when things looked impossible. That's made anything possible.

Finally, my wonderful wife, Carissa, and my daughters, Ana and Lisa, have my eternal gratitude and love. They gave up a lot of weekends and evenings so that I could hammer away in the office writing. Every time I got stuck, Carissa's constant reassurance that I'd "figure it out" always seemed to make it better. I am extremely lucky to have them in my corner.

Preface

Three months on the Web is like a year in real time.

Web developers pretty much think this way, since we're always hearing about something new. A year ago HTML5 and CSS3 seemed so far off in the distance, but already companies are using these technologies in their work today, because browsers like Google Chrome, Safari, Firefox, and Opera are starting to implement pieces of the specification.

HTML5 and CSS3 help lay the groundwork for the next generation of web applications. They let us build sites that are simpler to develop, easier to maintain, and more user-friendly. HTML5 has new elements for defining site structure and embedding content, which means we don't have to resort to extra markup or plug-ins. CSS3 provides advanced selectors, graphical enhancements, and better font support that makes our sites more visually appealing without using font image replacement techniques, complex Java-Script, or graphics tools. Improved accessibility support will improve Ajax applications for people with disabilities, and offline support lets us start building working applications that don't need an Internet connection.

In this book, you're going to find out about all of the ways you can use HTML5 and CSS3 right now, even if your users don't have browsers that can support all of these features yet. Before we get started, let's take a second and talk about HTML5 and buzzwords.

HTML5: The Platform vs. the Specification

HTML5 is a specification that describes some new tags and markup, as well as some wonderful JavaScript APIs, but it's getting caught up in a whirlwind of hype and promises. Unfortunately, HTML5 the standard has evolved into HTML5 the platform, creating an awful lot of confusion among developers, customers, and even authors. In some cases, pieces from the CSS3 specification such as shadows, gradients, and transformations are being called "HTML." Browser makers are trying to one-up each other with how much "HTML5" they support. People are starting to make strange requests like "My site will be in HTML5, right?"

For the majority of the book, we'll focus on the HTML5 and CSS3 specifications themselves and how you can use the techniques they describe. In the last part of the book, we'll look into a suite of closely related specifications that were once part of HTML5 but are in use right now on multiple platforms. These include Web SQL Databases, Geolocation, and Web Sockets. Although these things aren't *technically* HTML5, they can help you build incredible things when combined with HTML5 and CSS3.

How This Works

Each chapter in this book focuses on a specific group of problems that we can solve with HTML5 and CSS3. Each chapter has an overview and a table summarizing the tags, features, or concepts covered in the chapter. The main content of each chapter is broken apart into "tips," which introduce you to a specific concept and walk you through building a simple example using the concept. The chapters in this book are grouped topically. Rather than group things into an HTML5 part and a CSS3 part, it made more sense to group them based on the problems they solve.

Each tip contains a section called "Falling Back," which shows you methods for addressing the users who use browsers that don't offer HTML5 and CSS3 support. We'll be using a variety of techniques to make these fallbacks work, from third-party libraries to our own jQuery plug-ins. These tips can be read in any order you like.

Finally, each chapter wraps up with a section called "The Future," where we discuss how the concept can be applied as it becomes more widely adopted.

This book focuses on what you can use today. There are more HTML5 and CSS3 features that aren't in widespread use yet. You'll learn more about them in the final chapter, Chapter 11, *Where to Go Next*, on page 201.

What's in This Book

We'll start off with a brief overview of HTML5 and CSS3 and take a look at some of the new structural tags you can use to describe your page content. Then we'll work with forms, and you'll get a chance to use some of the form fields and features such as autofocus and placeholders. From there, you'll get to play with CSS3's new selectors so you can learn how to apply styles to elements without adding extra markup to your content.

Then we'll explore HTML's audio and video support, and you'll learn how to use the canvas to draw shapes. You'll also get to see how to use CSS3's shadows, gradients, and transformations, as well as how to learn how to work with fonts.

In the last section, we'll use HTML5's client-side features such as Web Storage, Web SQL Databases, and offline support to build client-side applications. We'll use Web Sockets to talk to a simple chat service, and you'll see how HTML5 makes it possible to send messages and data across domains. You'll also get a chance to play with the Geolocation API and learn how to manipulate the browser's history. We'll then wrap up by taking a look at a few things that aren't immediately useful but will become important in the near future.

In Appendix 1, *Features Quick Reference*, on page 215, you'll find a listing of all the features covered in this book with a quick reference to those chapters that reference those features. We'll be using a lot of jQuery in this book, so Appendix 2, *jQuery Primer*, on page 223, gives you a short primer. You'll also find a small appendix explaining how to encode audio and video files for use with HTML5.

Prerequisites

This book is aimed primarily at web developers who have a good understanding of HTML and CSS. If you're just starting out, you'll still find this book valuable, but I recommend you check out *Designing with Web Standards* [Zel09] and my book, *Web Design for Developers* [Hog09].

I also assume that you have a basic understanding of JavaScript and jQuery,[1] which we will be using to implement many of our fallback solutions. Appendix 2, *jQuery Primer*, on page 223, is a brief introduction to jQuery that covers the basic methods we'll be using.

You'll need Firefox 3.6, Google Chrome 5, Opera 10.6, or Safari 5 to test the code in this book. You'll probably need all of these browsers to test everything we'll be building, since each browser does things a little differently.

You'll also need a way to test your sites with Internet Explorer so you can ensure that the fallback solutions we create actually work. If you need to be able to test your examples in multiple versions of Internet Explorer, you can download IETester for Windows, because it supports IE 6, 7, and 8 in a single application. If you're not running Windows, you should consider using a

---

1. http://www.jquery.com

virtual machine like VirtualBox or VMware or using a service like Cross-BrowserTesting[2] or MogoTest.[3]

Online Resources

The book's website[4] has links to an interactive discussion forum as well as errata for the book. You can also find the source code for all the examples in this book linked on that page. Additionally, readers of the eBook can click on the gray box above the code excerpts to download that snippet directly

If you find a mistake, please create an entry on the Errata page so we can get it addressed. If you have an electronic copy of this book, there are links in the footer of each page that you can use to easily submit errata.

Finally, be sure to visit this book's blog, Beyond HTML5 and CSS3.[5] I'll be posting related material, updates, and working examples from this book.

Ready to go? Great! Let's get started with HTML5 and CSS3.

---

2. http://crossbrowsertesting.com/
3. http://www.mogotest.com/
4. http://www.pragprog.com/titles/bhh5/
5. http://www.beyondhtml5andcss3.com/

CHAPTER 1

An Overview of HTML5 and CSS3

HTML5[1] and CSS3[2] are more than just two new standards proposed by the World Wide Web Consortium (W3C) and its working groups. They are the next iteration of technologies you use every day, and they're here to help you build better modern web applications. Before we dive into the deep details of HTML5 and CSS3, let's talk about some benefits of HTML5 and CSS3, as well as some of the challenges we'll face.

1.1 A Platform for Web Development

A lot of the new features of HTML center around creating a better platform for web-based applications. From more descriptive tags and better cross-site and cross-window communication to animations and improved multimedia support, developers using HTML5 have a lot of new tools to build better user experiences.

More Descriptive Markup

Each version of HTML introduces some new markup, but never before have there been so many new additions that directly relate to describing content. You'll learn about elements for defining headings, footers, navigation sections, sidebars, and articles in Chapter 2, *New Structural Tags and Attributes*, on page 11. You'll also learn about meters, progress bars, and how custom data attributes can help you mark up data.

---

1. The HTML5 specification is at http://www.w3.org/TR/html5/.
2. CSS3 is split across multiple modules, and you can follow its progress at http://www.w3.org/Style/CSS/current-work.

Multimedia with Less Reliance on Plug-ins

You don't need Flash or Silverlight for video, audio, and vector graphics anymore. Although Flash-based video players are relatively simple to use, they don't work on Apple's mobile devices. That's a significant market, so you'll need to learn how to use non-Flash video alternatives. In Chapter 7, *Embedding Audio and Video*, on page 109, you'll see how to use HTML5 audio and video with effective fallbacks.

Better Applications

Developers have tried all kinds of things to make richer, more interactive applications on the Web, from ActiveX controls to Flash. HTML5 offers amazing features that, in some cases, completely eliminate the need for third-party technologies.

Cross-Document Messaging

Web browsers prevent us from using scripts on one domain to affect or interact with scripts on another domain. This restriction keeps end users safe from cross-site scripting, which has been used to do all sorts of nasty things to unsuspecting site visitors.

However, this prevents *all* scripts from working, even when we write them ourselves and know we can trust the content. HTML5 includes a workaround that is both safe and simple to implement. You'll see how to make this work in Tip 24, *Talking Across Domains*, on page 183.

Web Sockets

HTML5 offers support for Web Sockets, which give you a persistent connection to a server. Instead of constantly polling a back end for progress updates, your web page can subscribe to a socket, and the back end can push notifications to your users. We'll play with that a bit in Tip 25, *Chatting with Web Sockets*, on page 190.

Client-Side Storage

We tend to think of HTML5 as a web technology, but with the addition of the Web Storage and Web SQL Database APIs, we can build applications in the browser that can persist data entirely on the client's machine. You'll see how to use those APIs in Chapter 9, *Working with Client-Side Data*, on page 155.

Better Interfaces

The user interface is such an important part of web applications, and we jump through hoops every day to make browsers do what we want. To style a table or round corners, we either use JavaScript libraries or add tons of additional markup so we can apply styles. HTML5 and CSS3 make that practice a thing of the past.

Better Forms

HTML5 promises better user interface controls. For ages, we've been forced to use JavaScript and CSS to construct sliders, calendar date pickers, and color pickers. These are all defined as real elements in HTML5, just like dropdowns, checkboxes, and radio buttons. You'll learn about how to use them in Chapter 3, *Creating User-Friendly Web Forms*, on page 31. Although this isn't quite ready yet for every browser, it's something you need to keep your eye on, especially if you develop web-based applications. In addition to improved usability without reliance on JavaScript libraries, there's another benefit—improved accessibility. Screen readers and other browsers can implement these controls in specific ways so that they work easily for the disabled.

Improved Accessibility

Using the new HTML5 elements in HTML5 to clearly describe our content makes it easier for programs like screen readers to easily consume the content. A site's navigation, for example, is much easier to find if you can look for the nav tag instead of a specific div or unordered list. Footers, sidebars, and other content can be easily reordered or skipped altogether. Parsing pages in general becomes much less painful, which can lead to better experiences for people relying on assistive technologies. In addition, new attributes on elements can specify the roles of elements so that screen readers can work with them easier. In Chapter 5, *Improving Accessibility*, on page 79, you'll learn how to use those new attributes so that today's screen readers can use them.

Advanced Selectors

CSS3 has selectors that let you identify odd and even rows of tables, all selected check boxes, or even the last paragraph in a group. You can accomplish more with less code and less markup. This also makes it much easier to style HTML you can't edit. In Chapter 4, *Making Better User Interfaces with CSS3*, on page 55, you'll see how to use these selectors effectively.

Visual Effects

Drop shadows on text and images help bring depth to a web page, and gradients can also add dimension. CSS3 lets you add shadows and gradients to elements without resorting to background images or extra markup. In addition, you can use transformations to round corners or skew and rotate elements. You'll see how all of those things work in Chapter 8, *Eye Candy*, on page 127.

1.2 Backward Compatibility

One of the best reasons for you to embrace HTML5 today is that it works in most existing browsers. Right now, even in Internet Explorer 6, you can start using HTML5 and slowly transition your markup. It'll even validate with the W3C's validation service (conditionally, of course, because the standards are still evolving).

If you've worked with HTML or XML, you've come across the doctype declaration before. It's used to tell validators and editors what tags and attributes you can use and how the document should be formed. It's also used by a lot of web browsers to determine how the browser will render the page. A valid doctype often causes browsers to render pages in "standards mode."

Compared to the rather verbose *XHTML 1.0 Transitional* doctype used by many sites:

```
<!DOCTYPE html PUBLIC "-//W3C//DTD XHTML 1.0 Transitional//EN"
  "http://www.w3.org/TR/xhtml1/DTD/xhtml1-transitional.dtd">
```

the HTML5 doctype is ridiculously simple:

```
html5_why/index.html
<!DOCTYPE html>
```

Place that at the top of the document, and you're using HTML5.

Of course, you can't use any of the new HTML5 elements that your target browsers don't yet support, but your document will validate as HTML5.

1.3 The Road to the Future Is Bumpy

There are a few roadblocks that continue to impede the widespread adoption of HTML5 and CSS3. Some are obvious, and some are less so.

Internet Explorer

Internet Explorer currently has the largest user base, and versions 8 and below have very weak HTML5 and CSS3 support. IE 9 improves this situation, but it's not widely used yet. That doesn't mean we can't use HTML5 and CSS3 in our sites anyway. We can make our sites work in Internet Explorer, but they don't have to work the same as the versions we develop for Chrome and Firefox. We'll just provide fallback solutions so we don't anger users and lose customers.

Joe asks:

But I Like My XHTML Self-Closing Tags. Can I Still Use Them?

You sure can! Many developers fell in love with XHTML because of the stricter requirements on markup. XHTML documents forced quoted attributes, made you self-close content tags, required that you use lowercase attribute names, and brought well-formed markup onto the World Wide Web. Moving to HTML5 doesn't mean you have to change your ways. HTML5 documents will be valid if you use the HTML5-style syntax or the XHTML syntax, but you need to understand the implications of using self-closing tags.

Most web servers serve HTML pages with the text/html MIME type because of Internet Explorer's inability to properly handle the application/xml+xhtml MIME type associated with XHTML pages. Because of this, browsers tend to strip off self-closing tags because self-closing tags were not considered valid HTML before HTML5. For example, if you had a self-closing script tag above a div like this:

```
<script language="javascript" src="application.js" />
<h2>Help</h2>
```

the browser would remove the self-closing forward slash, and then the renderer would think that the h2 was *within* the script tag, *which never closes!* This is why you see script tags coded with an explicit closing tag, even though a self-closing tag is valid XHTML markup.

So, be aware of possible issues like this if you do use self-closing tags in your HTML5 documents, because they will be served with the text/html MIME type. You can learn more about this issue and others at http://www.webdevout.net/articles/beware-of-xhtml#myths.

Accessibility

Our users must be able to interact with our websites, whether they are visually impaired, hearing impaired, on older browsers, on slow connections, or on mobile devices. HTML5 introduces some new elements, such as audio, video, and canvas. Audio and video have always had accessibility issues, but the canvas element presents new challenges. The canvas element lets us create vector images within the HTML document using JavaScript. This creates issues for the visually impaired but also causes problems for the 5 percent of web users who have disabled JavaScript.[3]

We need to be mindful of accessibility when we push ahead with new technologies and provide suitable fallbacks for these HTML5 elements, just like we would for people using Internet Explorer.

---

3. http://visualrevenue.com/blog/2007/08/eu-and-us-javascript-disabled-index.html

Cake and Frosting

I like cake. I like pie better, but cake is pretty good stuff. I prefer cake with frosting on it.

When you're developing web applications, you have to keep in mind that all the pretty user interfaces and fancy JavaScript stuff is the frosting on the cake. Your website can be really good without that stuff, and just like a cake, you need a foundation on which to put your frosting.

I've met some people who don't like frosting. They scrape it off the cake. I've also met people who use web applications without JavaScript for varying reasons.

Bake these people a really awesome cake. Then add frosting.

Deprecated Tags

HTML5 has introduced a lot of new elements, but the specification also deprecates quite a few common elements that you might find in your web pages.[4] You'll want to remove those moving forward.

First, several presentational elements are gone. If you find these in your code, get rid of them! Replace them with semantically correct elements and use CSS to make them look nice.

- basefont
- big
- center
- font
- s
- strike
- tt
- u

Some of those tags are pretty obscure, but you will find a lot of pages out there maintained with visual editors such as Dreamweaver that still contain a lot of font and center tags.

Aside from the presentational elements, support for frames has been removed. Frames have always been popular in enterprise web applications such as PeopleSoft, Microsoft Outlook Web Access, and even custom-built portals. Despite the widespread use, frames caused so many usability and accessibility issues that they just had to go. That means these elements are gone:

---

4. http://www.w3.org/TR/html5-diff/

- frame
- frameset
- noframes

You should be looking at ways to lay out your interfaces without frames, using regular CSS or some JavaScript. If you're using frames to ensure the same header, footer, and navigation appears on each page of your application, you should be able to accomplish the same thing with the tools provided by your web development framework. A few other elements are gone because there are better options available:

- acronym gets replaced by abbr.
- applet gets replaced by object.
- dir gets replaced by ul.

In addition to deprecated elements, there are many attributes that are no longer valid. These include presentational attributes such as the following:

- align
- link, vlink, alink, and text attributes on the body tag
- bgcolor
- height and width
- scrolling on the iframe element
- valign
- hspace and vspace
- cellpadding, cellspacing, and border on table

If you use target on your links, like this:

```
<a href="http://www.google.com" target="_blank">
```

you'll want to look at using JavaScript instead, because target is deprecated.

The profile attribute on the head tag is no longer supported either, and this is something you tend to see in a lot of WordPress templates.

Finally, the longdesc attribute for img and iframe elements is gone, which is a bit of a disappointment to accessibility advocates, because longdesc was an accepted way of providing additional descriptive information to users of screen readers.

If you plan on using HTML5 with your existing sites, you'll want to look for these elements and remove them or replace them with more semantic ones.

Be sure to validate your pages with the W3C Validator service,[5] because this will help you locate deprecated tags and attributes.

Competing Corporate Interests

Internet Explorer is not the only browser slowing adoption of HTML5 and CSS3. Google, Apple, and the Mozilla Foundation have their own agendas as well, and they're battling it out for supremacy. They're arguing over video and audio codec support, and they're including their opinions in their browser releases. For example, Safari will play MP3 audio with the audio element, but ogg files won't work. Firefox, however, supports ogg files instead of mp3 files.

Eventually these differences will be resolved. In the meantime, we can make smart choices about what we support either by limiting what we implement to the browsers used by our target audiences or by implementing things multiple times, once for each browser until the standards are finalized. It's not as painful as it sounds. We'll discuss this more in Chapter 7, *Embedding Audio and Video*, on page 109.

HTML5 and CSS3 Are Still Works in Progress

They're not final specifications, and that means anything in those specifications could change. While Firefox, Chrome, and Safari have strong HTML5 support, if the specification changes, the browsers will change with it, and this could lead to some deprecated, broken websites. During the course of writing this book, CSS3 box shadows have been removed and re-added to the specification, and the Web Sockets protocol has been modified, breaking client-server communications entirely.

If you follow the progress of HTML5 and CSS3 and stay up-to-date with what's happening, you'll be fine. A good portion of the things we'll be discussing in this book are going to work for a long time.

When you come across something that doesn't work in one of your target browsers, you just fill in the gaps as you go, using JavaScript and Flash as your putty. You'll build solid solutions that work for all our users, and as time goes on, you'll be able to remove the JavaScript and other fallback solutions without changing your implementations.

But before you think too much about the future, let's start working with HTML5. There are a bunch of new structural tags waiting to meet you over in the next chapter. So, let's not keep them waiting, shall we?

---

5.   http://validator.w3.org/

Part I

Improving User Interfaces

CHAPTER 2

New Structural Tags and Attributes

In the first few chapters of this book, we'll talk about how we can use HTML5's and CSS's features to improve the interfaces we present to our users. We'll see how we can create better forms, easily style tables, and improve the accessibility of our pages for assistive devices. We'll also see how we can use content generation to improve the usability of our print style sheets, and we'll explore in-place editing with the new contenteditable attribute. First, though, let's take a look at how HTML5's new elements can help us structure our pages better.

I'd like to talk to you about a serious problem affecting many web developers today. *Divitis*—a chronic syndrome that causes web developers to wrap elements with extra div tags with IDs such as banner, sidebar, article, and footer—is rampant. It's also highly contagious. Developers pass Divitis to each other extremely quickly, and since divs are invisible to the naked eye, even mild cases of Divitis may go unnoticed for years.

Here's a common symptom of Divitis:

```
<div id="navbar_wrapper">
  <div id="navbar">
    <ul>
      <li><a href="/">Home</a></li>
      <li><a href="/">Home</a></li>
    </ul>
  </div>
</div>
```

Here we have an unordered list, which is already a block element,[1] wrapped with two div tags that are also block elements. The id attributes on these

---

1. Remember, block elements fall on their own line, whereas inline elements do not force a line break.

wrapper elements tell us what they do, but you can remove at least one of these wrappers to get the same result. Overuse of markup leads to bloat and pages that are difficult to style and maintain.

There is hope, though. The HTML5 specification provides a cure in the form of new semantic tags that describe the content they contain. Because so many developers have made sidebars, headers, footers, and sections in their designs, the HTML5 specification introduces new tags specifically designed to divide a page into logical regions. Let's put those new elements to work. Together with HTML5, we can help wipe out Divitis in our lifetime.

In addition to these new structural tags, we'll also talk about the meter element and discuss how we can use the new custom attributes feature in HTML5 so we can embed data into our elements instead of hijacking classes or existing attributes. In a nutshell, we're going to find out how to use the right tag for the right job.

In this chapter, we'll explore these new elements and features:[2]

<header>

Defines a header region of a page or section. *[C5, F3.6, IE8, S4, O10]*

<footer>

Defines a footer region of a page or section. *[C5, F3.6, IE8, S4, O10]*

<nav>

Defines a navigation region of a page or section. *[C5, F3.6, IE8, S4, O10]*

<section>

Defines a logical region of a page or a grouping of content. *[C5, F3.6, IE8, S4, O10]*

<article>

Defines an article or complete piece of content. *[C5, F3.6, IE8, S4, O10]*

<aside>

Defines secondary or related content. *[C5, F3.6, IE8, S4, O10]*

---

2. In the descriptions that follow, browser support is shown in square brackets using a shorthand code and the minimum supported version number. The codes used are *C:* Google Chrome, *F:* Firefox, *IE:* Internet Explorer, *O:* Opera, *S:* Safari, *IOS:* iOS devices with Mobile Safari, and *A:* Android Browser.

Custom data attributes

Allows the addition of custom attributes to any elements that use the data- pattern. *[All browsers support reading these via JavaScript's getAttribute() method.]*

<meter>

Describes an amount within a range. *[C5, F3.5, S4, O10]*

<progress>

Control that shows real-time progress toward a goal. *[Unsupported at publication time.]*

Tip 1

Redefining a Blog Using Semantic Markup

One place you're sure to find lots of content in need of structured markup is a blog. You're going to have headers, footers, multiple types of navigation (archives, blogrolls, and internal links), and, of course, articles or posts. Let's use HTML5 markup to mock up the front page of the blog for AwesomeCo, a company on the cutting edge of Awesomeness.

To get an idea of what we're going to build, take a look at Figure 1, *The blog structure using HTML5 semantic markup*, on page 15. It's a fairly typical blog structure, with a main header with horizontal navigation below the header. In the main section, each article has a header and a footer. An article may also have a pull quote, or an aside. There's a sidebar that contains additional navigation elements. Finally, the page has a footer for contact and copyright information. There's nothing new about this structure, except that this time, instead of coding it up with lots of div tags, we're going to use specific tags to describe these regions.

When we're all done, we'll have something that looks like Figure 2, *The finished layout*, on page 16.

It All Starts with the Right Doctype

We want to use HTML5's new elements, and that means we need to let browsers and validators know about the tags we'll be using. Create a new page called index.html, and place this basic HTML5 template into that file.

html5newtags/index.html
```
Line 1 <!DOCTYPE html>
    2 <html lang="en-US">
    3   <head>
    4     <meta http-equiv="Content-Type" content="text/html; charset=utf-8">
    5     <title>AwesomeCo Blog</title>
    6   </head>
    7
    8   <body>
    9   </body>
   10 </html>
```

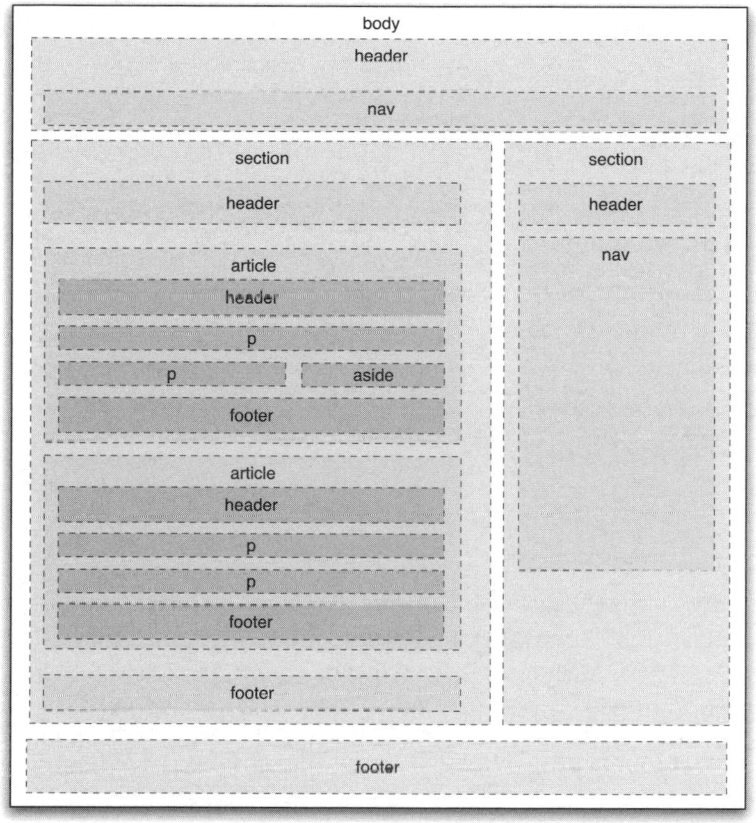

Figure 1—The blog structure using HTML5 semantic markup

Take a look at the doctype on line 1 of that example. This is all we need for an HTML5 doctype. If you're used to doing web pages, you're probably familiar with the long, hard-to-remember doctypes for XHTML like this:

```
<!DOCTYPE html PUBLIC "-//W3C//DTD XHTML 1.0 Transitional//EN"
  "http://www.w3.org/TR/xhtml1/DTD/xhtml1-transitional.dtd">
```

Now, take another look at the HTML5 doctype:

```
<!DOCTYPE html>
```

That's much simpler and much easier to remember.

The point of a doctype is twofold. First, it's to help validators determine what validation rules it needs to use when validating the code. Second, a doctype forces Internet Explorer versions 6, 7, and 8 to go into "standards mode," which is vitally important if you're trying to build pages that work across all

AwesomeCo Blog!

Latest Posts   Archives   Contributors   Contact Us

How Many Should We Put You Down For?

Posted by Brian on October 1st, 2010 at 2:39PM

The first big rule in sales is that if the person leaves empty-handed, they're likely not going to come back. That's why you have to be somewhat aggressive when you're working with a customer, but you have to make sure you don't overdo it and scare them away.

"Never give someone a chance to say no when selling your product."

One way you can keep a conversation going is to avoid asking questions that have yes or no answers. For example, if you're selling a service plan, don't ever ask "Are you interested in our 3 or 5 year service plan?" Instead, ask "Are you interested in the 3 year service plan or the 5 year plan, which is a better value?" At first glance, they appear to be asking the same thing, and while a customer can still opt out, it's harder for them to opt out of the second question because they have to say more than just "no."

25 Comments ...

Archives

- October 2010
- September 2010
- August 2010
- July 2010
- June 2010
- May 2010
- April 2010
- March 2010
- February 2010
- January 2010

© 2010 AwesomeCo.

Home   About   Terms of Service   Privacy

Figure 2—The finished layout

browsers. The HTML5 doctype satisfies both of these needs and *is even recognized by Internet Explorer 6.*

Headers

Headers, not to be confused with headings such as h1, h2, and h3, may contain all sorts of content, from the company logo to the search box. Our blog header will contain only the blog's title for now.

```
html5newtags/index.html
Line 1  <header id="page_header">
     2    <h1>AwesomeCo Blog!</h1>
     3  </header>
```

You're not restricted to having just one header on a page. Each individual section or article can also have a header, so it can be helpful to use the ID attribute like I did on 1 to uniquely identify your elements. A unique ID makes it easy to style elements with CSS or locate elements with JavaScript.

Footers

The footer element defines footer information for a document or an adjacent section. You've seen footers before on websites. They usually contain information like the copyright date and who owns the site. The specification says we

---

Semantic Markup

Semantic markup is all about describing your content. If you've been developing web pages for a few years, you've probably divided your pages into various regions such as header, footer, and sidebar so that you could more easily identify the regions of the page when applying style sheets and other formatting.

Semantic markup makes it easy for machines and people alike to understand the meaning and context of the content. The new HTML5 markup tags such as section, header, and nav help you do just that.

---

can have multiple footers in a document too, so that means we could use the footers within our blog articles too.

For now, let's just define a simple footer for our page. Since we can have more than one footer, we'll give this one an ID just like we did with the header. It'll help us uniquely identify this particular footer when we want to add styles to this element and its children.

`html5newtags/index.html`

```
<footer id="page_footer">
  <p>&copy; 2010 AwesomeCo.</p>
</footer>
```

This footer simply contains a copyright date. However, like headers, footers on pages often contain other elements, including navigational elements.

Navigation

Navigation is vital to the success of a website. People simply aren't going to stick around if you make it too hard for them to find what they're looking for, so it makes sense for navigation to get its own HTML tag.

Let's add a navigation section to our document's header. We'll add links to the blog's home page, the archives, a page that lists the contributors to the blog, and a link to a contact page.

Like headers and footers, your page can have multiple navigation elements. You often find navigation in your header and in your footer, so now you can identify those explicitly. Our blog's footer needs links to the AwesomeCo home page, the company's "about us" page, and links to the company's terms of service and privacy policies. We'll add these as another unordered list within the page's footer element.

```
html5newtags/index.html
<footer id="page_footer">
  <p>&copy; 2010 AwesomeCo.</p>
  <nav>
    <ul>
      <li><a href="http://awesomeco.com/">Home</a></li>
      <li><a href="about">About</a></li>
      <li><a href="terms.html">Terms of Service</a></li>
      <li><a href="privacy.html">Privacy</a></li>
    </ul>
  </nav>
</footer>
```

We will use CSS to change how both of these navigation bars look, so don't worry too much about the appearance yet. The point of these new elements is to describe the content, not to describe how the content looks.

Sections and Articles

Sections are the logical regions of a page, and the section element is here to replace the abused div tag when it comes to describing logical sections of a page.

```
html5newtags/index.html
<section id="posts">
</section>
```

Don't get carried away with sections, though. Use them to logically group your content! Here we've created a section that will hold all the blog posts. However, each post shouldn't be in its own section. We have a more appropriate tag for that.

Articles

The article tag is the perfect element to describe the actual content of a web page. With so many elements on a page, including headers, footers, navigational elements, advertisements, widgets, social media bookmarks, and blogrolls, it might be easy to forget that people come to your site because they're interested in the content you're providing. The article tag helps you describe that content.

Each of our articles will have a header, some content, and a footer. We can define an entire article like this:

```
html5newtags/index.html
<article class="post">
  <header>
    <h2>How Many Should We Put You Down For?</h2>
```

Joe asks:

What's the Difference Between Articles and Sections?

Think of a section as a logical part of a document. Think of an article as actual content, such as a magazine article, blog post, or news item.

These new tags describe the content they contain. Sections can have many articles, and articles can also have many sections. A section is like the sports section of a newspaper. The sports section has many articles. Each of those articles may again be divided into its own bunch of sections. Some sections like headers and footers have proper tags. A section is a more generic element you can use to logically group other elements.

Semantic markup is all about conveying the *meaning* of your content.

```html
  <p>Posted by Brian on
    <time datetime="2010-10-01T14:39">October 1st, 2010 at 2:39PM</time>
  </p>
</header>
<p>
  The first big rule in sales is that if the person leaves empty-handed,
  they're likely not going to come back. That's why you have to be
  somewhat aggressive when you're working with a customer, but you have
  to make sure you don't overdo it and scare them away.
</p>
<p>
  One way you can keep a conversation going is to avoid asking questions
  that have yes or no answers. For example, if you're selling a service
  plan, don't ever ask &quot;Are you interested in our 3 or 5 year
  service plan?&quot; Instead, ask &quot;Are you interested in the 3
  year service plan or the 5 year plan, which is a better value?&quot;
  At first glance, they appear to be asking the same thing, and while
  a customer can still opt out, it's harder for them to opt out of
  the second question because they have to say more than just
  &quot;no.&quot;
</p>
<footer>
  <p><a href="comments"><i>25 Comments</i></a> ...</p>
</footer>
</article>
```

We can use header and footer elements inside of our articles, which makes it much easier to describe those specific sections. We can also divide our article into multiple sections using the section element.

Asides and Sidebars

Sometimes you have content that adds something extra to your main content, such as pullout quotes, diagrams, additional thoughts, or related links. You can use the new aside tag to identify these elements.

html5newtags/index.html

```html
<aside>
  <p>
    &quot;Never give someone a chance to say no when
    selling your product.&quot;
  </p>
</aside>
```

We'll place the callout quote in an aside element. We'll nest this aside within the article, keeping it close to its related content.

Our completed section, with the aside, looks like this:

html5newtags/index.html

```html
<section id="posts">
  <article class="post">
    <header>
      <h2>How Many Should We Put You Down For?</h2>
      <p>Posted by Brian on
        <time datetime="2010-10-01T14:39">October 1st, 2010 at 2:39PM</time>
      </p>
    </header>
    <aside>
      <p>
        &quot;Never give someone a chance to say no when
        selling your product.&quot;
      </p>
    </aside>
    <p>
      The first big rule in sales is that if the person leaves empty-handed,
      they're likely not going to come back. That's why you have to be
      somewhat aggressive when you're working with a customer, but you have
      to make sure you don't overdo it and scare them away.
    </p>
    <p>
      One way you can keep a conversation going is to avoid asking questions
      that have yes or no answers. For example, if you're selling a service
      plan, don't ever ask &quot;Are you interested in our 3 or 5 year
      service plan?&quot; Instead, ask &quot;Are you interested in the 3
      year service plan or the 5 year plan, which is a better value?&quot;
      At first glance, they appear to be asking the same thing, and while
      a customer can still opt out, it's harder for them to opt out of
      the second question because they have to say more than just
      &quot;no.&quot;
    </p>
```

```
    <footer>
      <p><a href="comments"><i>25 Comments</i></a> ...</p>
    </footer>
  </article>
</section>
```

Now we just have to add the sidebar section.

Asides Are Not Page Sidebars!

Our blog has a sidebar on the right side that contains links to the archives for the blog. If you're thinking that we could use the aside tag to define the sidebar of our blog, you'd be wrong. You *could* do it that way, but it goes against the spirit of the specification. The aside is designed to show content related to an article. It's a good place to show related links, a glossary, or a pullout quote.

To mark up our sidebar that contains our list of prior archives, we'll just use another section tag and a nav tag.

html5newtags/index.html
```
<section id="sidebar">
  <nav>
    <h3>Archives</h3>
    <ul>
      <li><a href="2010/10">October 2010</a></li>
      <li><a href="2010/09">September 2010</a></li>
      <li><a href="2010/08">August 2010</a></li>
      <li><a href="2010/07">July 2010</a></li>
      <li><a href="2010/06">June 2010</a></li>
      <li><a href="2010/05">May 2010</a></li>
      <li><a href="2010/04">April 2010</a></li>
      <li><a href="2010/03">March 2010</a></li>
      <li><a href="2010/02">February 2010</a></li>
      <li><a href="2010/01">January 2010</a></li>
    </ul>
  </nav>
</section>
```

That's it for our blog's structure. Now we can start applying styles to these new elements.

Styling

We can apply styles to these new elements just like we'd style div tags. First, we create a new style sheet file called style.css and attach it to our HTML document by placing a style sheet link in the header, like this:

html5newtags/index.html
```
<link rel="stylesheet" href="style.css" type="text/css">
```

Let's first center the page's content and set some basic font styles.

html5newtags/style.css
```
body{
  width:960px;
  margin:15px auto;
  font-family: Arial, "MS Trebuchet", sans-serif;
}

p{
  margin:0 0 20px 0;
}

p, li{
  line-height:20px;
}
```

Next, we define the header's width.

html5newtags/style.css
```
header#page_header{
  width:100%;
}
```

We style the navigation links by transforming the bulleted lists into horizontal navigation bars.

html5newtags/style.css
```
header#page_header nav ul, footer#page_footer nav ul{
  list-style: none;
  margin: 0;
  padding: 0;
}

header#page_header nav ul li, footer#page_footer nav ul li{
  padding:0;
  margin: 0 20px 0 0;
  display:inline;
}
```

The posts section needs to be floated left and given a width, and we also need to float the callout inside the article. While we're doing that, let's bump up the font size for the callout.

html5newtags/style.css
```
section#posts{
  float: left;
  width: 74%;
}
```

```
section#posts aside{
  float: right;
  width: 35%;
  margin-left: 5%;
  font-size: 20px;
  line-height: 40px;
}
```

We'll also need to float the sidebar and define its width.

html5newtags/style.css
```
section#sidebar{
  float: left;
  width: 25%;
}
```

And we need to define the footer. We'll clear the floats on the footer so that it sits at the bottom of the page.

html5newtags/style.css
```
footer#page_footer{
  clear: both;
  width: 100%;
  display: block;
  text-align: center;
}
```

These are just basic styles. From here, I'm confident you can make this look much, much better.

Falling Back

Although this all works great in Firefox, Chrome, and Safari, the people in management aren't going to be too happy when they see the mess that Internet Explorer makes out of our page. The content displays fine, but since IE doesn't understand these elements, it can't apply styles to them, and the whole page resembles something from the mid-1990s.

The only way to make IE style these elements is to use JavaScript to define the elements as part of the document. That turns out to be really easy. We'll add this code to our head section of the page so it executes before the browser renders any elements. We'll place it inside a *conditional comment*, a special type of comment that only Internet Explorer will read.

html5newtags/index.html
```
<!--[if lt IE 9]>
<script type="text/javascript">
  document.createElement("nav");
  document.createElement("header");
  document.createElement("footer");
```

```
    document.createElement("section");
    document.createElement("aside");
    document.createElement("article");
</script>
<![endif]-->
```

This particular comment targets any version of Internet Explorer older than version 9.0. If we reload our page, it looks correct now.

We are creating a dependency on JavaScript, though, so you need to take that into consideration. The improved organization and readability of the document make it worth it, and since there are no accessibility concerns, because the contents still display and are read by a screen reader, you're only making the presentation seem grossly out-of-date to your users who have disabled JavaScript intentionally.

This approach is fine for adding support for a handful of elements or for understanding how you can add support. Remy Sharp's brilliant HTMLShiv[3] takes this approach much further and might be more appropriate for incorporating fallback support if you're looking to support many more elements.

---

3. http://code.google.com/p/html5shiv/

Meters and Progress Bars

If you need to implement a pledge meter or an upload progress bar in a web application, you should investigate the meter and progress elements introduced in HTML5.

The meter element lets us semantically describe an actual fixed point on a meter with a minimum and maximum value. For your meter to be in harmony with the specification, you shouldn't use your meter for things with arbitrary minimum or maximum values like height and weight, unless you are talking about something specific where you have set a specific boundary. For example, if we have a fundraising website and we want to show how close we are to our goal of $5,000, we can describe that easily:

```
html5_meter/index.html
<section id="pledge">
  <header>
    <h3>Our Fundraising Goal</h3>
  </header>
  <meter title="USD" id="pledge_goal"
         value="2500" min="0" max="5000">
    $2500.00
  </meter>
  <p>Help us reach our goal of $5000!</p>
</section>
```

The progress element is very similar to a meter, but it's designed to show active progress like you'd see if you were uploading a file. A meter, by comparison, is designed to show a measurement that's not currently moving, like a snapshot of available storage space on the server for a given user. The markup for a progress bar is very similar to the meter element.

```
html5_meter/progress.html
<progress id="progressbar" max=100><span>0</span>%</progress>
```

The meter and progress elements aren't styled by any browsers yet, but you can use JavaScript to grab the values in the meter and build your own visualization, using the meter or progress to semantically describe the data. You can see an example of how you might do that by looking at the book's example files for the meter element.

Tip 2

Creating Pop-up Windows with Custom Data Attributes

If you've built any web application that uses JavaScript to grab information out of the document, you know that it can sometimes involve a bit of hackery and parsing to make things work. You'll end up inserting extra information into event handlers or abusing the rel or class attributes to inject behavior. Those days are now over thanks to the introduction of custom data attributes.

Custom data attributes all start with the prefix data- and are ignored by the validator for HTML5 documents. You can attach a custom data attribute to any element you'd like, whether it be metadata about a photograph, latitude and longitude coordinates, or, as you'll see in this tip, dimensions for a pop-up window. Best of all, you can use custom data attributes right now in nearly every web browser, since they can be easily grabbed with JavaScript.

Separating Behavior from Content, or Why onclick Is Bad

Over the years, pop-up windows have gotten a bad reputation, and often rightly so. They're often used to get you to look at an ad, to convince unsuspecting web surfers to install spyware or viruses, or, worse, to give away personal information that is then resold. It's no wonder most browsers have some type of pop-up blocker available.

Pop-ups aren't all bad, though. Web application developers often rely on pop-up windows to display online help, additional options, or other important user interface features. To make pop-ups less annoying, we need to implement them in an unobtrusive manner. When you look at AwesomeCo's human resources page, you see several links that display policies in pop-up windows. Most of them look like this:

```
html5_popups_with_custom_data/original_example_1.html
<a href='#'
  onclick="window.open('holiday_pay.html',WinName,'width=300,height=300');">
  Holiday pay
</a>
```

This is a pretty common way to build links that spawn pop-ups. In fact, this is the way JavaScript newbies often learn how to make pop-up windows.

There are a couple of problems that we should address with this approach before moving on, though.

Improve Accessibility

The link destination isn't set! If JavaScript is disabled, the link won't take the user to the page. That's a huge problem we need to address immediately. Do not *ever* omit the href attribute or give it a value like this under *any* circumstances. Give it the address of the resource that would normally pop up.

html5_popups_with_custom_data/original_example_2.html

```
<a href='holiday_pay.html'
  onclick="window.open(this.href,WinName,'width=300,height=300');">
  Holiday pay
</a>
```

The JavaScript code then reads the attached element's href attribute for the link's location.

The first step toward building accessible pages is to ensure that all the functionality works *without* JavaScript.

Abolish the onclick

Keep the behavior separate from the content, just like you keep the presentation information separate by using linked style sheets. Using onclick is easy at first, but imagine a page with fifty links, and you'll see how the onclick method gets out of hand. You'll be repeating that JavaScript over and over again. And if you generate this code from some server-side code, you're just increasing the number of JavaScript events and making the resulting HTML much bigger than it needs to be.

Instead, give each of the anchors on the page a class that identifies them.

html5_popups_with_custom_data/original_example_3.html

```
<a href="holiday_pay" class="popup">Holiday Pay</a>
```

html5_popups_with_custom_data/original_example_3.html

```
var links = $("a.popup");

links.click(function(event){
    event.preventDefault();
    window.open($(this).attr('href'));
});
```

We use a jQuery selector to grab the element with the class of popup, and then we add an observer to each element's click event. The code we pass to the click method will be executed when someone clicks the link. The preventDefault method prevents the default click event behavior. In this case, it prevents the browser from following the link and displaying a new page.

One thing we've lost, though, is the information on how to size and position the window, which is something we had in the original example. We want a page designer who isn't that familiar with JavaScript to still be able to set the dimensions of a window on a per-link basis.

Custom Data Attributes to the Rescue!

Situations like this are common when building any JavaScript-enabled application. As we've seen, storing the window's desired height and width with the code is desirable, but the onclick approach has lots of drawbacks. What we can do instead is embed these attributes as attributes on the element. All we have to do is construct the link like this:

html5_popups_with_custom_data/popup.html

```
<a href="help/holiday_pay.html"
   data-width="600"
   data-height="400"
   title="Holiday Pay"
   class="popup">Holiday pay</a>
```

Now we just modify the click event we wrote to grab the options from the custom data attributes of the link and pass them to the window.open method.

html5_popups_with_custom_data/popup.html

```
$(function(){
  $(".popup").click(function(event){
    event.preventDefault();
    var href = $(this).attr("href");
    var width = $(this).attr("data-width");
    var height = $(this).attr("data-height");
    var popup = window.open (href,"popup",
      "height=" + height +",width=" + width + "");
  });
});
```

That's all there is to it! The link now opens in a new window.

Falling Back

These attributes work in older browsers right now as long as they support JavaScript. The custom data attributes won't trip up the browser, and your document will be valid since you're using the HTML5 doctype, since the attributes that start with data- will all be ignored.

> ## A Word of Caution
>
> In this example, we used custom data attributes to provide additional information to a client-side script. It's a clever approach to a specific problem and illustrates one way to use these attributes. It does tend to mix presentation information with our markup, but it's a simple way to show you how easy it is to use JavaScript to read values you embed in your page.

2.1 The Future

We can do some interesting things with these new tags and attributes once they're widely supported. We can identify and disable navigation and article footers very easily using print style sheets.

```
nav, article>footer{display:none}
```

We can use scripting languages to quickly identify all of the articles on a page or on a site. But most important, we mark up content with appropriate tags that describe it so we can write better style sheets and better JavaScript.

Custom data attributes give developers the flexibility to embed all sorts of information in their markup. In fact, we'll use them again in Chapter 6, *Drawing on the Canvas*, on page 93.

You can use them with JavaScript to determine whether a form tag should submit via Ajax, by simply locating any form tag with data-remote=true, which is something that the Ruby on Rails framework is doing.

You can also use them to display dates and times in a user's time zone while still caching the page. Simply put the date on the HTML page as UTC, and convert it to the user's local time on the client side. These attributes allow you to embed real, usable data in your pages, and you can expect to see more and more frameworks and libraries taking advantage of them. I'm sure you'll find lots of great uses for them in your own work.

And we can help wipe out Divitis once and for all!

CHAPTER 3

Creating User-Friendly Web Forms

If you've ever designed a complicated user interface, you know how limiting the basic HTML form controls are. You're stuck using text fields, select menus, radio buttons, checkboxes, and sometimes the even clunkier *multiple select* lists that you constantly have to explain to your users how to use. ("Hold down the Ctrl key and click the entries you want, unless you're on a Mac, in which case use the Cmd key.")

So, you do what all good web developers do—you turn to Prototype or jQuery, or you roll your own controls and features using a combination of HTML, CSS, and JavaScript. But when you look at a form that has sliders, calendar controls, spinboxes, autocomplete fields, and visual editors, you quickly realize that you've created a nightmare for yourself. You'll have to make sure that the controls you include on your page don't conflict with any of the other controls you've included or any of the other JavaScript libraries on the page. You can spend hours implementing a calendar picker only to find out later that now the Prototype library is having problems because jQuery took over the $() function. So, you use jQuery's noConflict() method, but then you find out that the color picker control you used no longer works because that plug-in wasn't written carefully enough.

If you're smiling, it's because you've been there. If you're fuming, I'm guessing it's for the same reason. There is hope, though. In this chapter, we're going to build a couple of web forms using some new form field types, and we'll also implement autofocusing and placeholder text. Finally, we'll discuss how to use the new contenteditable attribute to turn any HTML field into a user input control.

Specifically, we'll cover the following features:[1]

Email field [<input type="email">]
:   Displays a form field for email addresses. *[O10.1, IOS]*

URL field [<input type="url">]
:   Displays a form field for URLs. *[O10.1, IOS]*

Telephone field [<input type="tel">]
:   Displays a form field for telephone numbers. *[O10.1, IOS]*

Search field [<input type="search">
:   Displays a form field for search keywords. *[C5, S4, O10.1, IOS]*

Slider (range) [<input type="range">]
:   Displays a slider control. *[C5, S4, O10.1]*

Number [<input type="number">]
:   Displays a form field for numbers, often as a spinbox. *[C5, S5, O10.1, IOS]*

Date fields [<input type="date">]
:   Displays a form field for dates. Supports date, month, or week. *[C5, S5, O10.1]*

Dates with Times [<input type="datetime">]
:   Displays a form field for dates with times. Supports datetime, datetime-local, or time. *[C5, S5, O10.1]*

Color [<input type="color">]
:   Displays a field for specifying colors. *[C5, S5]* (Chrome 5 and Safari 5 understand the Color field but do not display any specific control.)

Autofocus support [<input type="text" autofocus>]
:   Support for placing the focus on a specific form element. *[C5, S4]*

Placeholder support [<input type="email" placeholder="me@example.com">]
:   Support for displaying placeholder text inside of a form field. *[C5, S4, F4]*

In-place editing support [<p contenteditable>lorem ipsum</p>]
:   Support for in-place editing of content via the browser. *[C4, S3.2, IE6, O10.1]*

Let's start by learning about some of the extremely useful form field types.

---

1. In the descriptions that follow, browser support is shown in square brackets using a shorthand code and the minimum supported version number. The codes used are *C:* Google Chrome, *F:* Firefox, *IE:* Internet Explorer, *O:* Opera, *S:* Safari, *IOS:* iOS devices with Mobile Safari, and *A:* Android Browser.

Tip 3

Describing Data with New Input Fields

HTML5 introduces several new input types that you can use to better describe the type of data your users are entering. In addition to the standard text fields, radio buttons, and checkbox elements, you can use elements such as email fields, calendars, color pickers, spinboxes, and sliders. Browsers can use these new fields to display better controls to the user without the need for JavaScript. Mobile devices and virtual keyboards for tablets and touch-screens can use the field types to display different keyboard layouts. For example, the iPhone's Mobile Safari browser displays alternate keyboard layouts when the user is entering data into the URL and email types, making special characters like @ . : and / easily accessible.

Improving the AwesomeCo Projects Form

AwesomeCo is working on creating a new project management web application to make it easier for developers and managers to keep up with the progress of the many projects they have going on. Each project has a name, a contact email address, and a staging URL so managers can preview the website as it's being built. There are also fields for the start date, priority, and estimated number of hours the project should take to complete. Finally, the development manager would like to give each project a color so he can quickly identify each project when he looks at reports.

Let's mock up a quick project preferences page using the new HTML5 fields.

Setting Up the Basic Form

Let's create a basic HTML form that does a POST request. Since there's nothing special about the name field, we'll use the trusty text field.

```
html5forms/index.html
<form method="post" action="/projects/1">

  <fieldset id="personal_information">
    <legend>Project Information</legend>
    <ol>
      <li>
        <label for="name">Name</label>
        <input type="text" name="name" autofocus id="name">
      </li>
```

```
    <li>
      <input type="submit" value="Submit">
    </li>
  </ol>

  </fieldset>

</form>
```

Notice that we are marking this form up with labels wrapped in an ordered list. Labels are essential when creating accessible forms. The for attribute of the label references the id of its associated form element. This helps screen readers identify fields on a page. The ordered list provides a good way of listing the fields without resorting to complex table or div structures. This also gives you a way to mark up the order in which you'd like people to fill out the fields.

Creating a Slider Using Range

Sliders are commonly used to let users decrease or increase a numerical value and could be a great way to quickly allow managers to both visualize and modify the priority of the project. You implement a slider with the range type.

html5forms/index.html
```
<label for="priority">Priority</label>
<input type="range" min="0" max="10"
       name="priority" value="0" id="priority">
```

Add this to the form, within a new li element just like the previous field.

Chrome and Opera both implement a Slider widget, which looks like this:

Priority

Notice that we've also set the min and max range for the slider. That will constrain the value of the form field.

Handling Numbers with Spinboxes

We use numbers a lot, and although typing numbers is fairly simple, spinboxes can make making minor adjustments easier. A spinbox is a control with arrows that increment or decrement the value in the box. Let's use the spinbox for estimated hours. That way, the hours can be easily adjusted.

html5forms/index.html
```
<label for="estimated_hours">Estimated Hours</label>
<input type="number" name="estimated_hours"
       min="0" max="1000"
       id="estimated_hours">
```

Opera supports the spinbox control, which looks like this:

Estimated Hours

The spinbox also allows typing by default, and like range sliders, we can set minimum and maximum values. However, those minimum and maximum ranges won't be applied to any value you type into the field.

Also notice that you can control the size of the increment step by giving a value to the step parameter. It defaults to 1 but can be any numerical value.

Dates

Recording the start date of the project is pretty important, and we want to make that as easy as possible. The date input type is a perfect fit here.

```
html5forms/index.html
<label for="start_date">Start date</label>
<input type="date" name="start_date" id="start_date"
       value="2010-12-01">
```

At the time of writing, Opera is the only browser that currently supports a full calendar picker.

Here's an example of its implementation:

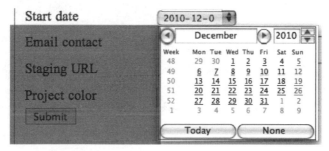

Safari 5.0 displays a field similar to the number field with arrows to increment and decrement the date. It defaults to "1582" if left blank. Other browsers render a text field.

Email

The HTML5 specification says that the email input type is designed to hold either a single email address or an email address list, so that's the perfect candidate for our email field.

```
html5forms/index.html
<label for="email">Email contact</label>
<input type="email" name="email" id="email">
```

Mobile devices get the most benefit from this type of form field, because the virtual keyboard layouts change to make entering email addresses easier.

URL

There's a field type designed to handle URLs too. This one is especially nice if your visitor uses an iPhone, because it displays a much different keyboard layout, displaying helper buttons for quickly entering web addresses, similar to the keyboard displayed when entering a URL into Mobile Safari's address bar. Adding the staging URL field is as simple as adding this code:

```
html5forms/index.html
<label for="url">Staging URL</label>
<input type="url" name="url" id="url">
```

Virtual keyboards use this field type to display a different layout as well.

Color

Finally, we need to provide a way to enter a color code, and we'll use the color type for that.

```
html5forms/index.html
<label for="project_color">Project color</label>
<input type="color" name="project_color" id="project_color">
```

At the time of writing, no browsers display a color picker control, but that shouldn't stop you from using this field. You're using proper markup to describe your content, and that's going to come in handy in the future, especially when you need to provide fallback support.

Opera supports most of these new controls right now, as you can see in Figure 3, *Some form controls are already supported in Opera.*, on page 37, but when you open the page in Firefox, Safari, or Google Chrome, you won't see much of a difference. We'll need to fix that.

Falling Back

Browsers that don't understand these new types simply fall back to the text type, so your forms will still be usable. At that point, you can bind one of the jQuery UI or YUI widgets to that field to transform it. As time goes on and more browsers support these controls, you can remove the JavaScript hooks.

Replacing the Color Picker

We can easily identify and replace the color picker using jQuery with CSS3's attribute selectors. We locate any input field with the type of color and apply a jQuery plug-in called SimpleColor.

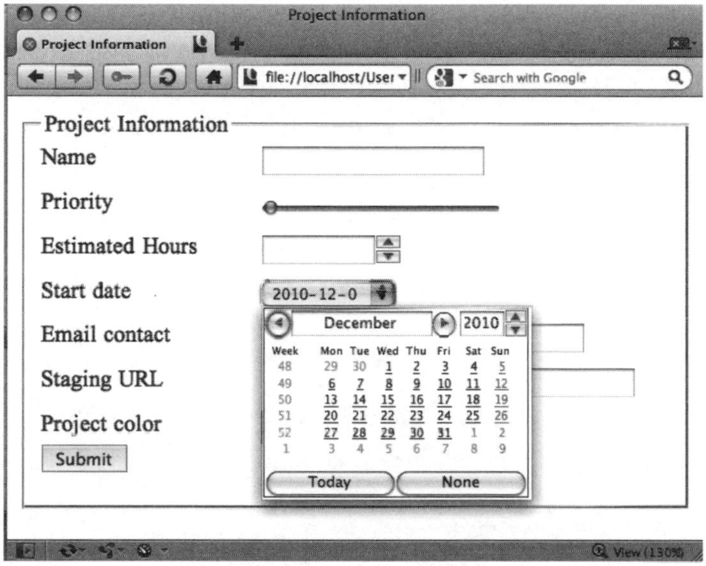

Figure 3—Some form controls are already supported in Opera.

html5forms/index.html

```
if (!hasColorSupport()){
  $('input[type=color]').simpleColor();
}
```

Since we used the new form types in our markup, we don't have to add an additional class name or other markup to identify the color pickers. Attribute selectors and HTML5 go together quite well.

We don't want to use this color picker plug-in if the browser has native support for it, so we will use some JavaScript to detect whether the browser supports input fields with a type of color.

html5forms/index.html

```
Line 1 function hasColorSupport(){
        input = document.createElement("input");
        input.setAttribute("type", "color");
        var hasColorType = (input.type !== "text");
     5  // handle Safari/Chrome partial implementation
        if(hasColorType){
          var testString = "foo";
          input.value=testString;
          hasColorType = (input.value != testString);
    10  }
        return(hasColorType);
      }
```

First, we use plain JavaScript to create an element and set its type attribute to color. Then, we retrieve the type attribute to see whether the browser allowed us to set the attribute. If it comes back with a value of color, then we have support for that type. If not, we'll have to apply our script.

Things get interesting on line 6. Safari 5 and Google Chrome 5 have partially implemented the color type. They support the field, but they don't actually display a color widget. We still end up with a text field on the page. So, in our detection method, we set the value for our input field and see whether the value sticks around. If it doesn't, we can assume that the browser has implemented a color picker because the input field isn't acting like a text box.

The whole bit of code to replace the color picker looks like this:

```
html5forms/index.html
if (!hasColorSupport()){
  $('input[type=color]').simpleColor();
}
```

That solution works, but it's very brittle. It targets a specific set of browsers and only for the color control. Other controls have their own quirks that you need to learn. Thankfully, there's an alternative solution.

Modernizr

The Modernizr[2] library can detect support for many HTML5 and CSS3 features. It doesn't add the missing functionality, but it does provide several mechanisms similar to the solution we implemented for detecting form fields that are more bulletproof.

Before you start throwing Modernizr in your projects, be sure you take some time to understand how it works. Whether you wrote the code yourself or not, if you use it in your project, you're responsible for it. Modernizr wasn't ready to handle Safari's partial support of the color field right away. When the next version of Chrome or Firefox comes out, you may have to hack together a solution. Who knows, maybe you'll be able to contribute that solution back to Modernizr!

You'll implement fallbacks for controls such as the date picker and the slider in the same manner. Sliders and date pickers are included as components in the jQuery UI library.[3] You'll include the jQuery UI library on the page, detect whether the browser supports the control natively, and, if it doesn't, apply the JavaScript version instead. Eventually you'll be able to phase out

---

2.   http://www.modernizr.com/
3.   http://jqueryui.com/

the JavaScript controls and rely completely on the controls in the browser. Because of the complexity involved with detecting these types, Modernizer will be very helpful to you. However, we'll continue writing our own detection techniques throughout the rest of this book so you can see how they work.

Aside from new form field types, HTML5 introduces a few other attributes for form fields that can help improve usability. Let's take a look at autofocus next.

Tip 4

Jumping to the First Field with Autofocus

You can really speed up data entry if you place the user's cursor in the first field on the form when they load the page. Many search engines do this using JavaScript, and now HTML5 provides this capability as part of the language.

All you have to do is add the autofocus attribute to any form field, like we did on the profile page in Tip 3, *Describing Data with New Input Fields*, on page 33.

```
html5forms/index.html
<label for="name">Name</label>
<input type="text" name="name" autofocus id="name">
```

You can have only one autofocus attribute on a page for it to work reliably. If you have more than one, the browser will focus the user's cursor onto the last autofocused form field.

Falling Back

We can detect the presence of the autofocus attribute with a little bit of Java-Script and then use jQuery to focus on the element when the user's browser doesn't have autofocus support. This is probably the easiest fallback solution you'll come across.

```
html5forms/autofocus.js
function hasAutofocus() {
  var element = document.createElement('input');
  return 'autofocus' in element;
}
$(function(){
  if(!hasAutofocus()){
    $('input[autofocus]').focus();
  }
});
```

Just include this JavaScript on your page, and you'll have autofocus support where you need it.

Autofocus makes it a little easier for users to start working with your forms when they load, but you may want to give them a little more information about the type of information you'd like them to provide. Let's take a look at the placeholder attribute next.

Tip 5

Providing Hints with Placeholder Text

Placeholder text provides users with instructions on how they should fill in the fields. A sign-up form with placeholder text is shown in Figure 4, *Placeholders can help users understand what you're asking them to do.*, on page 42. We're going to construct that form now.

A Simple Sign-Up Form

AwesomeCo's support site requires users to sign up for an account, and one of the biggest problems with the sign-ups is that users keep trying to use insecure passwords. Let's use placeholder text to give users a little guidance on our password requirements. For consistency's sake, we'll add placeholder text to the other fields too.

To add placeholder text, you just add the placeholder attribute to each input field, like this:

html5placeholdertext/index.html
```
<input id="email" type="email"
       name="email" placeholder="user@example.com">
```

Our entire form's markup looks something like this, with placeholder text for each field:

html5placeholdertext/index.html
```
<form id="create_account" action="/signup" method="post">

  <fieldset id="signup">
    <legend>Create New Account</legend>

    <ol>
      <li>
        <label for="first_name">First Name</label>
        <input id="first_name" type="text"
               autofocus="true"
               name="first_name" placeholder="'John'">
      </li>
      <li>
        <label for="last_name">Last Name</label>
        <input id="last_name" type="text"
               name="last_name" placeholder="'Smith'">
      </li>
```

Figure 4—Placeholders can help users understand what you're asking them to do.

```html
<li>
  <label for="email">Email</label>
  <input id="email" type="email"
         name="email" placeholder="user@example.com">
</li>
<li>
  <label for="password">Password</label>
  <input id="password" type="password" name="password" value=""
         autocomplete="off" placeholder="8-10 characters" />
</li>
<li>
  <label for="password_confirmation">Password Confirmation</label>
  <input id="password_confirmation" type="password"
         name="password_confirmation" value=""
         autocomplete="off" placeholder="Type your password again" />
</li>
<li><input type="submit" value="Sign Up"></li>
      </ol>
   </fieldset>
</form>
```

Preventing Autocompletion

You may have noticed we've added the autocomplete attribute to the password fields on this form. HTML5 introduces an autocomplete attribute that tells web browsers that they should not attempt to automatically fill in data for the field. Some browsers remember data that users have previously typed in, and in some cases, we want to tell the browsers that we'd rather not let users do that.

Since we're once again using the ordered list element to hold our form fields, we'll add a bit of basic CSS to make the form look nicer.

```
html5placeholdertext/style.css
fieldset{
  width: 216px;
}

fieldset ol{
  list-style: none;
  padding:0;
  margin:2px;
}

fieldset ol li{
  margin:0 0 9px 0;
  padding:0;
}

/* Make inputs go to their own line */
fieldset input{
  display:block;
}
```

Now, users of Safari, Opera, and Chrome will have helpful text inside the form fields. Now let's make Firefox and Internet Explorer play along.

Falling Back

You can use JavaScript to put placeholder text on form fields without too much work. You test the value of each form field, and if it's empty, you set its value to the placeholder value. When the form receives focus, you clear out the value, and when the field loses focus, you test the value again. If it's different, you leave it alone, and if it's empty, you replace it with the placeholder text.

You test for placeholder support just like you test for autofocus support.

```
html5placeholdertext/index.html
function hasPlaceholderSupport() {
  var i = document.createElement('input');
  return 'placeholder' in i;
}
```

Then you just write your JavaScript to handle the changes. We'll use a solution based on work by Andrew January[4] and others to make this work. We'll fill in the values of all form fields with the text stored in the placeholder attribute. When a user selects a field, we'll remove the text we placed in the field. Let's wrap this up in a jQuery plug-in so that it's easy to apply the behavior to our form. See *jQuery Plug-ins*, on page 46 to learn how plug-ins work.

html5placeholdertext/jquery.placeholder.js

```
Line 1  (function($){

          $.fn.placeholder = function(){

     5      function valueIsPlaceholder(input){
              return ($(input).val() == $(input).attr("placeholder"));
            }
            return this.each(function() {

    10        $(this).find(":input").each(function(){

                if($(this).attr("type") == "password"){

                  var new_field = $("<input type='text'>");
    15            new_field.attr("rel", $(this).attr("id"));
                  new_field.attr("value", $(this).attr("placeholder"));
                  $(this).parent().append(new_field);
                  new_field.hide();

    20            function showPasswordPlaceHolder(input){
                    if( $(input).val() == "" || valueIsPlaceholder(input) ){
                      $(input).hide();
                      $('input[rel=' + $(input).attr("id") + ']').show();
                    };
    25          };

                  new_field.focus(function(){
                    $(this).hide();
                    $('input#' + $(this).attr("rel")).show().focus();
    30          });

                  $(this).blur(function(){
                      showPasswordPlaceHolder(this);
                  });
    35
                  showPasswordPlaceHolder(this);

                }else{
```

---

4. The original script is at http://www.morethannothing.co.uk/wp-content/uploads/2010/01/placeholder.js but didn't support password fields in IE.

```
40        // Replace the value with the placeholder text.
          // optional reload parameter solves FF and
          // IE caching values on fields.
          function showPlaceholder(input, reload){
            if( $(input).val() == "" ||
45          ( reload && valueIsPlaceholder(input) ) ){
                $(input).val($(input).attr("placeholder"));
            }
          };

50        $(this).focus(function(){
            if($(this).val() == $(this).attr("placeholder")){
              $(this).val("");
            };
          });
55
          $(this).blur(function(){
              showPlaceholder($(this), false)
          });

60        showPlaceholder(this, true);
        };
      });

      // Prevent forms from submitting default values
65    $(this).submit(function(){
        $(this).find(":input").each(function(){
          if($(this).val() == $(this).attr("placeholder")){
            $(this).val("");
          }
70      });
      });

    });
  };
75
})(jQuery);
```

There are a couple of interesting things in this plug-in that you should know about. On line 45, we're reloading the placeholder text into the fields if they have no value but also if we've refreshed the page. Firefox and other browsers persist the values of forms. We're setting the value attribute to the placeholder, and we certainly don't want that to accidentally become the user's actual value. When we load the page, we pass true to this method, which you can see on line 60.

Password fields behave a little differently than other form fields, so we have to handle those differently as well. Take a look at line 12. We're detecting the

jQuery Plug-ins

You can extend jQuery by writing your own plug-ins. You add your own methods to the jQuery function, and your plug-in seamlessly becomes available to any developer who includes your library. Here's a really trivial example that displays a JavaScript alert box:

```
jQuery.fn.debug = function() {
  return this.each(function(){
    alert(this.html());
  });
```

If you wanted to see a pop-up box appear for every paragraph on the page, you'd call it like this:

```
$("p").debug();
```

jQuery plug-ins are designed to iterate over a collection of jQuery objects, and they also return that object collection so that you can chain them. For example, since our debug plug-in also returns the jQuery collection, we can use jQuery's css method to change the color of the text of these paragraphs, all on one line.

```
$("p").debug().css("color", "red");
```

We'll make use of jQuery plug-ins a few times throughout this book to help us keep our code organized when we create fallback solutions. You can learn more at jQuery's documentation site.[a]

---

a.   http://docs.jquery.com/Plugins/Authoring

presence of a password field, and we have to change its type to a regular text field so that the value doesn't show up masked with asterisks. Some browsers throw errors if you try to convert password fields, so we'll have to swap out the password field for a text field. We'll swap those fields in and out as the user interacts with the fields.

This hack changes the values on the forms, and you probably want to prevent those placeholders from making their way back to the server. Since we're hacking in this placeholder code only when JavaScript is enabled, we can use JavaScript to inspect the form submission and strip out any values that match the placeholder text. On line 65, we capture the form submission and clear out the values of any input fields that equal the placeholder values.

Now that it's all written up as a plug-in, we can invoke it on the page by attaching it to the form like this:

html5placeholdertext/index.html

```
$(function(){
  function hasPlaceholderSupport() {
    var i = document.createElement('input');
    return 'placeholder' in i;
  }

  if(!hasPlaceholderSupport()){
    $("#create_account").placeholder();
    //END placeholder_fallback

    $('input[autofocus=true]').focus();
  };
});
```

Now we have a pretty decent solution that makes placeholder text a viable option for your web apps, no matter what browser you use.

Tip 6

In-Place Editing with contenteditable

We're always looking for ways to make it easier for people to interact with our applications. Sometimes we want a user of our site to edit information about themselves without having to navigate to a different form. We traditionally implement in-place editing by watching text regions for clicks and replacing those regions with text fields. These fields send the changed text back to the server via Ajax. HTML5's contenteditable tag takes care of the data-entry part automatically. We'll still have to write some JavaScript to send the data back to the server so we can save it, but we no longer have to create and toggle hidden forms.

One of AwesomeCo's current projects lets users review their account profile. It displays their name, city, state, postal code, and email address. Let's add some in-place editing to this profile page so that we end up with an interface like Figure 5, *In-place editing made easy*, on page 49.

Before we get started, I want you to know that implementing a feature that relies on JavaScript without first implementing a server-side solution goes against everything I believe in when it comes to building accessible web applications. We're doing it this way here because I want to focus on the features of the contenteditable attribute, *and this is not production code*. Always, and I mean *always*, build the solution that does not require JavaScript, *then* build the version that relies on scripting, and finally be sure to write automated tests for both paths so that you're more likely to catch bugs if you change one version and not the other.

The Profile Form

HTML5 introduces the contenteditable attribute that is available on almost every element. Simply adding this attribute turns it into an editable field.

```
html5_content_editable/show.html
<h1>User information</h1>
<div id="status"></div>
<ul>
  <li>
    <b>Name</b>
    <span id="name" contenteditable="true">Hugh Mann</span>
```

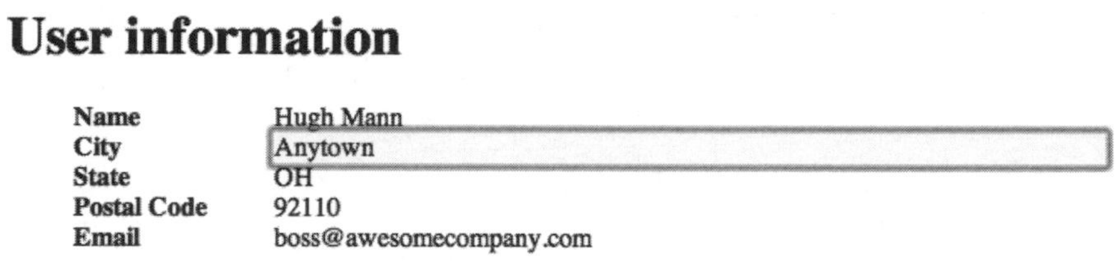

User information

Name	Hugh Mann
City	Anytown
State	OH
Postal Code	92110
Email	boss@awesomecompany.com

Figure 5—In-place editing made easy

```
      </li>
      <li>
        <b>City</b>
        <span id="city" contenteditable="true">Anytown</span>
      </li>
      <li>
        <b>State</b>
        <span id="state" contenteditable="true">OH</span>
      </li>
      <li>
        <b>Postal Code</b>
        <span id="postal_code" contenteditable="true">92110</span>
      </li>
      <li>
        <b>Email</b>
        <span id="email" contenteditable="true">boss@awesomecompany.com</span>
      </li>
    </ul>
```

We can style this up with some CSS too. We'll use some CSS3 selectors to identify the editable fields so they change color when our users hover over or select them.

html5_content_editable/show.html

```
Line 1  ul{list-style:none;}

      li{clear:both;}

   5  li>b, li>span{
        display: block;
        float: left;
        width: 100px;
      }
  10
      li>span{
        width:500px;
        margin-left: 20px;
      }
  15
```

```
li>span[contenteditable=true]:hover{
  background-color: #ffc;
}

li>span[contenteditable=true]:focus{
  background-color: #ffa;
  border: 1px shaded #000;
}
```

That's it for the front end. Users can modify the data on the page easily. Now we have to save it.

Persisting the Data

Although the users can change the data, their changes will be lost if they refresh the page or navigate away. We need a way to submit those changes to our back end, and we can do that easily with jQuery. If you've ever done any Ajax before, this won't be anything new to you.

html5_content_editable/show.html
```
$(function(){
    var status = $("#status");
    $("span[contenteditable=true]").blur(function(){
      var field = $(this).attr("id");
      var value = $(this).text();
      $.post("http://localhost:4567/users/1",
          field + "=" + value,
          function(data){
            status.text(data);
          }
      );
    });
});
```

We'll add an event listener to every span on the page that has the contenteditable attribute set to true. Then, all we have to do is submit the data to our server-side script.

Falling Back

We've done a bunch of things that won't work for some of our audience. First, we've created a dependency on JavaScript to save the edited results back to the server, which is a Bad Thing. Next, we're using the focus pseudoclass to highlight the fields when they receive focus, and some versions of IE don't support that. Let's handle the functionality first, and then we'll deal with the visual effects.

Creating an Edit Page

Rather than worrying too much about various situations that might prevent a user from using our technique, let's just give them the option to go to a separate page with its own form. Sure, it's more coding, but think about the possible scenarios:

- A user doesn't have JavaScript turned on and is using Internet Explorer 7.

- A user doesn't have an HTML5-compatible browser.

- A user is using the latest Firefox with HTML5 support but still disabled JavaScript simply because they don't like JavaScript (it happens all the time...more than you'd think).

When it comes down to it, making a form that does a POST to the same action that handled the Ajax update makes the most sense. How you do this is up to you, but many frameworks let you detect the type of request by looking at the accept headers to determine whether the request came from a regular POST or an XMLHttpRequest. That way, you keep the server-side code DRY.[6] We'll hide the link to this form if the browser supports contenteditable and JavaScript.

So, create a new page called edit.html, and code up a standard edit form that posts to the same update action that our Ajax version uses.

```
html5_content_editable/edit.html
<!DOCTYPE html>
<html lang="en-US">
  <head>
    <meta http-equiv="Content-Type" content="text/html; charset=utf-8">
    <title>Editing Profile</title>
    <link href="style.css" rel="stylesheet" media="screen">
  </head>
  <body>
    <form action="/users/1" method="post" accept-charset="utf-8">
      <fieldset id="your_information">
        <legend>Your Information</legend>
        <ol>
        <li>
          <label for="name">Your Name</label>
          <input type="text" name="name" value="" id="name">
        </li>
        <li>
          <label for="city">City</label>
          <input type="text" name="city" value="" id="city">
        </li>
```

---

6. DRY stands for "Don't Repeat Yourself" and is a term coined by Dave Thomas and Andy Hunt in *The Pragmatic Programmer* [HT00].

```
    <li>
      <label for="state">State</label>
      <input type="text" name="state" value="" id="state">
    </li>
    <li>
      <label for="postal_code">Postal Code</label>
      <input type="text" name="postal_code" value="" id="postal_code">
    </li>
    <li>
      <label for="email">Email</label>
      <input type="email" name="email" value="" id="email">
    </li>
  </ol>

</fieldset>
<p><input type="submit" value="Save"></p>
</form>

</body>
</html>
```

Then, add a link to this page on show.html.

html5_content_editable/show.html

```
<h1>User information</h1>
<section id="edit_profile_link">
  <p><a href="edit.html">Edit Your Profile</a></p>
</section>
<div id="status"></div>
```

With the link added, we just need to modify our script a bit. We want to hide the link to the edit page and enable the Ajax support only if we have support for editable content.

html5_content_editable/show.html

```
if(document.getElementById("edit_profile_link").contentEditable != null){
```

With the detection in place, our script looks like this:

html5_content_editable/show.html

```
$(function(){
  if(document.getElementById("edit_profile_link").contentEditable != null){
    $("#edit_profile_link").hide();
    var status = $("#status");
    $("span[contenteditable=true]").blur(function(){
      var field = $(this).attr("id");
      var value = $(this).text();
      $.post("http://localhost:4567/users/1",
          field + "=" + value,
          function(data){
            status.text(data);
```

```
      }
    );
  });
  }
});
```

With that in place, our users have the ability to use a standard interface or a quicker "in-place" mode. Now that you know how to implement this interface, remember to implement the fallback solution first. Unlike the other fallback solutions, this particular one cripples functionality if not implemented.

3.1 The Future

Right now, if you add a JavaScript-based date picker to your site, your users have to learn how it works. If you've ever shopped online for plane tickets and made hotel reservations, you're already familiar with the different ways people implement custom form controls on sites. It's akin to using an ATM—the interface is often different enough to slow you down.

Imagine, though, if each website used the HTML5 date field, and the browser had to create the interface. Each site a user visited would display the exact same date picker. Screen-reading software could even implement a standard mechanism to allow the blind to enter dates easily. Now think about how useful placeholder text and autofocus can be for users once it's everywhere. Placeholder text can help screen readers explain to users how form fields should work, and autofocus could help people navigate more easily without a mouse, which is handy for the blind but also for users with motor impairments who may not use the mouse.

The ability for developers to turn any element into an editable region makes it easy to do in-place editing, but it could potentially change how we build interfaces for content management systems.

The modern Web is all about interactivity, and forms are an essential part of that interactivity. The enhancements provided by HTML5 give us a whole new set of tools we can use to help our users.

CHAPTER 4

Making Better User Interfaces with CSS3

For far too long, we developers have hacked around CSS to get the effects we need in our code. We've used JavaScript or server-side code to stripe table rows or put focus and blur effects on our forms. We've had to litter our tags with additional class attributes just so we could identify which of our fifty form inputs we want to style.

But no more! CSS3 has some amazing selectors that make some of this work trivial. In case you forgot, a selector is a pattern that you use to help you find elements in the HTML document so you can apply styles to those elements. We'll use these new selectors to style a table. Then we'll take a look at how we can use some other CSS3 features to improve our site's print style sheets, and we'll split content into multiple columns.

We'll look at these CSS features in this chapter:[1]

:nth-of-type [p:nth-of-type(2n+1){color: red;}]
> Finds all n elements of a certain type. *[C2, F3.5, S3, IE9, O9.5, IOS3, A2]*

:first-child [p:first-child{color:blue;}]
> Finds the first child element. *[C2, F3.5, S3, IE9, O9.5, IOS3, A2]*

:nth-child [p:nth-child(2n+1){color: red;}]
> Finds a specific child element counting forward. *[C2, F3.5, S3, IE9, O9.5, IOS3, A2]*

:last-child [p:last-child{color:blue;}]
> Finds the last child element. *[C2, F3.5, S3, IE9, O9.5, IOS3, A2]*

---

1. In the descriptions that follow, browser support is shown in square brackets using a shorthand code and the minimum supported version number. The codes used are *C:* Google Chrome, *F:* Firefox, *IE:* Internet Explorer, *O:* Opera, *S:* Safari, *IOS:* iOS devices with Mobile Safari, and *A:* Android Browser.

:nth-last-child [p:nth-last-child(2){color: red;}]

> Finds a specific child element counting backward. *[C2, F3.5, S3, IE9, O9.5, IOS3, A2]*

:first-of-type [p:first-of-type{color:blue;}]

> Finds the first element of the given type. *[C2, F3.5, S3, IE9, O9.5, IOS3, A2]*

:last-of-type [p:last-of-type{color:blue;}]

> Finds the last element of the given type. *[C2, F3.5, S3, IE9, O9.5, IOS3, A2]*

Column support [#content{ column-count: 2; column-gap: 20px;
column-rule: 1px solid #ddccb5; }]

> Divides a content area into multiple columns. *[C2, F3.5, S3, O11.1, IOS3, A2]*

:after [span.weight:after { content: "lbs"; color: #bbb; }]

> Used with content to insert content after the specified element. *[C2, F3.5, S3, IE8, O9.5, IOS3, A2]*

Media Queries [media="only all and (max-width: 480)"]

> Apply styles based on device settings. *[C3, F3.5, S4, IE9, O10.1, IOS3, A2]*

Tip 7

Styling Tables with Pseudoclasses

A *pseudoclass* in CSS is a way to select elements based on information that lies outside the document or information that can't be expressed using normal selectors. You've probably used pseudoclasses like :hover before to change the color of a link when the user hovers over it with their mouse pointer. CSS3 has several new pseudoclasses that make locating elements much easier.

Improving an Invoice

AwesomeCo uses a third-party billing and invoicing system for products it ships. You see, one of AwesomeCo's biggest markets is conference swag, such as pens, cups, shirts, and anything else you can slap your logo on. You've been asked to make the invoice more readable. Right now, the developers are producing a standard HTML table that looks like the one in Figure 6, *The current invoice uses an unstyled HTML table.*, on page 58.

It's a pretty standard invoice with prices, quantities, row totals, a subtotal, a shipping total, and a grand total for the order. It would be easier to read if every other row were colored differently. It would also be helpful if the grand total was a different color so that it stands out more.

The code for the table looks like this. Copy it into your own file so you can work with it.

```
css3advancedselectors/table.html
<table >
  <tr>
    <th>Item</th>
    <th>Price</th>
    <th>Quantity</th>
    <th>Total</th>
  </tr>
  <tr>
    <td>Coffee mug</td>
    <td>$10.00</td>
    <td>5</td>
    <td>$50.00</td>
  </tr>
  <tr>
    <td>Polo shirt</td>
```

Item	Price	Quantity	Total
Coffee mug	$10.00	5	$50.00
Polo shirt	$20.00	5	$100.00
Red stapler	$9.00	4	$36.00
Subtotal			$186.00
Shipping			$12.00
Total Due			$198.00

Figure 6—The current invoice uses an unstyled HTML table.

```
    <td>$20.00</td>
    <td>5</td>
    <td>$100.00</td>
  </tr>
  <tr>
    <td>Red stapler</td>
    <td>$9.00</td>
    <td>4</td>
    <td>$36.00</td>
  </tr>
  <tr>
    <td colspan="3">Subtotal</td>
    <td>$186.00</td>
  </tr>
  <tr>
    <td colspan="3">Shipping</td>
    <td>$12.00</td>
  </tr>
  <tr>
    <td colspan="3">Total Due</td>
    <td>$198.00</td>
  </tr>
</table>
```

First, let's get rid of the hideous default table border.

css3advancedselectors/table.css
```
table{
  width: 600px;
  border-collapse: collapse;
}

th, td{
  border: none;
}
```

We'll also style the header a bit by giving it a black background with white text.

css3advancedselectors/table.css
```
th{
  background-color: #000;
  color: #fff;
}
```

Apply that style, and the table looks like this:

Item	Price	Quantity	Total
Coffee mug	$10.00	5	$50.00
Polo shirt	$20.00	5	$100.00
Red stapler	$9.00	4	$36.00
Subtotal			$186.00
Shipping			$12.00
Total Due			$198.00

With the table's borders and spacing cleaned up a bit, we can start using the pseudoclasses to style individual rows and columns. We'll start by striping the table.

Striping Rows with :nth-of-type

Adding "zebra striping" to tables is something we've all seen. It's useful because it gives users horizontal lines to follow. This kind of styling is best done in CSS, the presentation layer. That has traditionally meant adding additional class names to our table rows like "odd" and "even." We don't want to pollute our table's markup like that, because the HTML5 specification encourages us to avoid using class names that define presentation. Using some new selectors, we can get what we want without changing our markup at all, truly separating presentation from content.

The nth-of-type selector finds every *nth* element of a specific type using either a formula or keywords. We'll get into the formula in more detail soon, but first, let's focus on the keywords, because they're immediately easier to grasp.

We want to stripe every other row of the table with a different color, and the easiest way to do that is to find every even row of the table and give it a background color. We then do the same thing with the odd rows. CSS3 has even and odd keywords that support this exact situation.

css3advancedselectors/table.css
```
tr:nth-of-type(even){
  background-color: #F3F3F3;
}
```

```
tr:nth-of-type(odd) {
  background-color:#ddd;
}
```

So, this selector says, "Find me every even table row and color it. Then find every odd row and color that too." That takes care of our zebra striping, without resorting to any scripting or extra class names on rows.

With the styles applied, our table looks like this:

Item	Price	Quantity	Total
Coffee mug	$10.00	5	$50.00
Polo shirt	$20.00	5	$100.00
Red stapler	$9.00	4	$36.00
Subtotal			$186.00
Shipping			$12.00
Total Due			$198.00

Now let's work on aligning the columns in the table.

Aligning Column Text with :nth-child

By default, all of the columns in our invoice table are left-aligned. Let's right-align every column except for the first column. This way, our price and quantity columns will be right-aligned and easier to read. To do that, we can use nth-child, but first we have to learn how it works.

The nth-child selector looks for child elements of an element and, like nth-of-type, can use keywords or a formula.

The formula is an+b, where b is the offset, and a is a multiple. That description is not particularly helpful without some context, so let's look at it in the context of our table.

If we wanted to select all of the table rows, we could use this selector:

```
table tr:nth-child(n)
```

We're not using any multiple, nor are we using an offset.

However, if we wanted to select all rows of the table except for the first row, which is the row containing the column headings, we would use this selector that uses an offset:

```
table tr:nth-child(n+2)
```

If we wanted to select every other row of our table, we'd use a multiple, or 2n.

```
table tr:nth-child(2n)
```

If you wanted every third row, you'd use 3n.

You can also use the offset so that you can start further down the table. This selector would find every other row, starting with the fourth row:

```
table tr:nth-child(2n+4)
```

So, we can align every column *except* the first one with this rule:

```
css3advancedselectors/table.css
td:nth-child(n+2){
  text-align: right;
}
```

At this point, our table is really shaping up:

Item	Price	Quantity	Total
Coffee mug	$10.00	5	$50.00
Polo shirt	$20.00	5	$100.00
Red stapler	$9.00	4	$36.00
Subtotal			$186.00
Shipping			$12.00
Total Due			$198.00

Now, let's style the last row of the table.

Bolding the Last Row with :last-child

The invoice is looking pretty good right now, but one of the managers would like the bottom row of the table to be bolder than the other rows so it stands out more. We can use last-child for that too, which grabs the last child in a group.

Applying a bottom margin to paragraphs so that they are evenly spaced on a page is a common practice among many web developers. This can sometimes lead to an extra bottom margin at the end of a group, and that might be undesirable. For example, if the paragraphs are sitting inside of a sidebar or callout box, we may want to remove the bottom margin from the last paragraph so that there's not wasted space between the bottom of the last paragraph and the border of the box. The last-child selector is the perfect tool for this. We can use it to remove the margin from the last paragraph.

```
p{ margin-bottom: 20px }
#sidebar p:last-child{ margin-bottom: 0; }
```

Let's use this same technique to bold the contents of the last row.

css3advancedselectors/table.css
```
tr:last-child{
  font-weight: bolder;
}
```

Let's do the same thing with the last column of the table. This will help the line totals stand out too.

css3advancedselectors/table.css
```
td:last-child{
  font-weight: bolder;
}
```

Finally, we'll make the total's font size bigger by using last-child with descendant selectors. We'll find the last column of the last row and style it with this:

css3advancedselectors/table.css
```
tr:last-child td:last-child{
  font-size:24px;
}
```

Item	Price	Quantity	Total
Coffee mug	$10.00	5	$50.00
Polo shirt	$20.00	5	$100.00
Red stapler	$9.00	4	$36.00
Subtotal			$186.00
Shipping			$12.00
Total Due			$198.00

We're almost done, but there are a few things left to do with the last three rows of the table.

Counting Backward with :nth-last-child

We'd like to highlight the shipping row of the table when there's a discounted shipping rate. We'll use nth-last-child to quickly locate that row. You saw how you can use nth-child and the formula an+b to select specific child elements in *Aligning Column Text with :nth-child*, on page 60. The nth-last-child selector works exactly the same way, except that it counts backward through the children, starting at the last child first. This makes it easy to grab the second-to-last element in a group. It turns out we need to do just that with our invoice table.

So, to find our shipping row, we'd use this code:

css3advancedselectors/table.css
```
tr:nth-last-child(2){
  color: green;
}
```

Here, we're just specifying a specific child, the second to the last.

There's one last thing we should do with this table, though. Earlier, we right-aligned all the columns except for the first column, and although that looks fine for the rows of the table with the item descriptions and prices, it makes the last three rows of the table look a little funny. Let's right-align the bottom three rows as well. We can do that by using nth-last-child with a negative value for n and a positive value for a in our formula, like this:

```
css3advancedselectors/table.css
tr:nth-last-child(-n+3) td{
  text-align: right;
}
```

You can think of this as a range selector...it's using the offset of 3, and since we're using nth-last-child, it's grabbing every element before the offset. If you were using nth-child, this formula would grab every row up to the offset.

Our newly styled table, shown in Figure 7, *Our styled table, with striping and alignment done entirely with CSS3*, on page 64, looks much better now, and we didn't have to change the underlying markup one bit. Many of the selectors we used to accomplish this are not yet available to people using Internet Explorer, so we need a workaround for them.

Falling Back

Current versions of Opera, Firefox, Safari, and Chrome all understand these selectors, but Internet Explorer versions 8.0 and older will just ignore these entirely. You'll need a good fallback solution, and you have a choice to make.

Change the HTML Code

The most obvious solution that works everywhere is to modify the underlying code. You could attach classes to all the cells in the table and apply basic CSS to each class. This is the worst choice, because it mixes presentation and content and is exactly the kind of thing we're using CSS3 to avoid. Someday we wouldn't need all that extra markup, and it would be painful to remove it.

Use JavaScript

The jQuery library already understands most of the CSS3 selectors we used, so we could quickly write a method to style the table that way, but there's an easier way.

Item	Price	Quantity	Total
Coffee mug	$10.00	5	$50.00
Polo shirt	$20.00	5	$100.00
Red stapler	$9.00	4	$36.00
		Subtotal	$186.00
		Shipping	$12.00
		Total Due	$198.00

Figure 7—Our styled table, with striping and alignment done entirely with CSS3

Keith Clark has written a great little library called IE-css3[2] that adds support for CSS3 selectors to Internet Explorer. All we need to do is add a couple of scripts to our page.

The IE-CSS3 library can use jQuery, Prototype, or several other libraries under the hood, but I prefer to use the DOMAssistant[3] library because it has the best support for all the pseudoclasses we've used here.

Download both of those libraries, and then link them to your document. Since this is for IE only, you can place them in a conditional comment so they'll be used only by your IE users.

```
css3advancedselectors/table.html
<!--[if (gte IE 5.5)&(lte IE 8)]>
  <script type="text/javascript"
          src="js/DOMAssistantCompressed-2.8.js"></script>
  <script type="text/javascript"
          src="js/ie-css3.js"></script>
<![endif]-->
```

Placing those scripts in the page makes things look just great in Internet Explorer. You can see what it looks like in Figure 8, *Our table looks great in Internet Explorer.*, on page 65.

Although this will require the user to have JavaScript turned on, the table styling is mainly there to make the content easier to see. Lack of styling doesn't prevent anyone from reading the invoice.

Styling elements is a whole lot easier with CSS3, especially if we don't have the ability to modify the HTML we're targeting. When you're styling interfaces, use the semantic hierarchy and these new selectors before you add additional markup. You will find your code much easier to maintain.

---

2. http://www.keithclark.co.uk/labs/ie-css3/

3. http://www.domassistant.com/

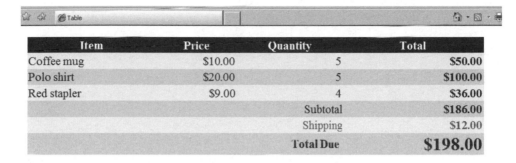

Item	Price	Quantity	Total
Coffee mug	$10.00	5	**$50.00**
Polo shirt	$20.00	5	**$100.00**
Red stapler	$9.00	4	**$36.00**
		Subtotal	**$186.00**
		Shipping	$12.00
		Total Due	**$198.00**

Figure 8—Our table looks great in Internet Explorer.

Tip 8

Making Links Printable with :after and content

CSS can style existing elements, but it can also inject content into a document. There are a few cases where content generation with CSS makes sense, and the most obvious one is appending the URL of a hyperlink next to the link's text when a user prints the page. When you're looking at a document on the screen, you can just hover over a link and see where it goes by looking at the status bar. However, when you look at a printout of a page, you have absolutely no idea where those links go.

AwesomeCo is working up a new page for its forms and policies, and one of the members of the redesign committee insists on printing out a copy of the site each time. He wants to be able to know exactly where all of the links go on the page so that he can determine whether they need to be moved. With just a little bit of CSS, we can add that functionality, and it will work in IE 8, Firefox, Safari, and Chrome. We can use some proprietary JavaScript to make it work in IE 6 and 7.

The page itself has nothing more than a list of links on it right now. Eventually it'll get put into a template.

css3_print_links/index.html

```
<ul>
  <li>
    <a href="travel/index.html">Travel Authorization Form</a>
  </li>
  <li>
    <a href="travel/expenses.html">Travel Reimbursement Form</a>
  </li>
  <li>
    <a href="travel/guidelines.html">Travel Guidelines</a>
  </li>
</ul>
</body>
```

If you were to look at that page on a printout, you'd have no idea where those links go. Let's fix that.

The CSS

When we add a style sheet to a page, we can specify the media type that the styles apply to. Most of the time, we use the screen type. However, we can use the print type to define a style sheet that loads only when the page is printed (or when the user uses the print preview function).

```
css3_print_links/index.html
<link rel="stylesheet" href="print.css" type="text/css" media="print">
```

We can then create a print.css style sheet file with this simple rule:

```
css3_print_links/print.css
a:after {
  content: " (" attr(href) ") ";
}
```

This takes every link on the page and adds the value of the href value inside parentheses after the link's text. When you print it from a modern browser, it looks just like this:

Forms and Policies

- Travel Authorization Form (travel/index.html)
- Travel Reimbursement Form (travel/expenses.html)
- Travel Guidelines (travel/guidelines.html)

If you want to see it in action without actually using up paper, you can use your browser's Print Preview feature, which also triggers this style sheet.

That handles everything except for Internet Explorer 6 and 7. Let's fix that, shall we?

Falling Back

Internet Explorer has a couple of JavaScript events that I wish every browser would adopt: onbeforeprint and onafterprint. Using those events, we can modify the hyperlink text when the printing is triggered and then revert the links when printing is finished. Our users will never notice the difference.[4]

We just need to create a file called print.js and add this code:

---

4. This technique is outlined nicely at http://beckelman.net/post/2009/02/16/Use-JQuery-to-Show-a-Linke28099s-Address-After-its-Text-When-Printing-In-IE6-and-IE7.aspx.

```
css3_print_links/print.js
Line 1  $(function() {
    -     if (window.onbeforeprint !== undefined) {
    -         window.onbeforeprint = ShowLinks;
    -         window.onafterprint = HideLinks;
    5     }
    - });

    -   function ShowLinks() {
    -     $("a").each(function() {
   10       $(this).data("linkText", $(this).text());
    -       $(this).append(" (" + $(this).attr("href") + ")");
    -     });
    -   }

   15  function HideLinks() {
    -     $("a").each(function() {
    -       $(this).text($(this).data("linkText"));
    -     });
    -   }
```

Then we just need to attach it to our page. We only need this fallback for IE
6 and 7, so we'll use a conditional comment for that. This code relies on
jQuery, so we have to make sure that we link in the jQuery library as well.

```
css3_print_links/index.html
  <script
    charset="utf-8"
    src='http://ajax.googleapis.com/ajax/libs/jquery/1.4.2/jquery.min.js'
    type='text/javascript'>
  </script>
  <!--[if lte IE 7]>
  <script type="text/javascript" src="print.js"></script>
  <![endif]-->
</head>
<body>
  <h1>Forms and Policies</h1>

    <ul>
      <li>
        <a href="travel/index.html">Travel Authorization Form</a>
      </li>
      <li>
        <a href="travel/expenses.html">Travel Reimbursement Form</a>
      </li>
      <li>
        <a href="travel/guidelines.html">Travel Guidelines</a>
      </li>
    </ul>
```

With the JavaScript linked, the link URLs will print on all of our target browsers. You can use this print style sheet as the basis for a more comprehensive one, and you may choose to apply this behavior to only some links on your site, not to every link like we did here.

Tip 9

Creating Multicolumn Layouts

The print industry has had columns for years, and web designers have looked at those publications with envy. Narrow columns make it easier for readers to read your content, and with displays getting wider, developers are looking for ways to preserve comfortable column widths. After all, nobody wants to follow multiple lines of text across the monitor any more than they want a line of text to flow across the whole page of a newspaper. There have been some pretty clever solutions in the past ten years, but none of those solutions are as simple and easy as the method provided by the CSS3 specification.

Splitting Columns

Each month, AwesomeCo publishes a newsletter for its employees. The company happens to use a popular web-based email system. Email-based newsletters don't quite look good and are very hard to maintain. They've decided to put the newsletter on the intranet site and are planning to just send emails to employees with a link to pull up the newsletter in their browsers. For a mocked-up version of this new newsletter, see Figure 9, *Our single-column newsletter is harder to read because it's very wide.*, on page 71.

The new director of communications, who has a background in print publications, has decided that she would like the newsletter to look more like an actual newsletter, with two columns instead of one.

If you've ever tried to split some text into multiple columns using divs and floats, you know how hard that can be. The first big hurdle you run into is that you have to manually decide where to split the text. In publishing software such as InDesign, you can "link" text boxes together so that when one fills up with text, the text flows into the linked text area. We don't have anything quite like that on the Web just yet, but we have something that works really well and is quite easy to use. We can take an element and split its contents into multiple columns, each with the same width.

We'll start with the markup for the newsletter. It's fairly basic HTML. Since its content will change once it's written, we're just going to use placeholder text for the content. If you're wondering why we're not using the new HTML5

AwesomeCo Newsletter

Volume 3, Issue 12

News From The Director

Lorem ipsum dolor sit amet, consectetur adipisicing elit, sed do eiusmod tempor incididunt ut labore et dolore magna aliqua. Ut enim ad minim veniam, quis nostrud exercitation ullamco laboris nisi ut aliquip ex ea commodo consequat.

Duis aute irure dolor in reprehenderit in voluptate velit esse cillum dolore eu fugiat nulla pariatur. Excepteur sint occaecat cupidatat non proident, sunt in culpa qui officia deserunt mollit anim id est laborum.

Quick Bits of Awesome

Lorem ipsum dolor sit amet, consectetur adipisicing elit, sed do eiusmod tempor incididunt ut labore et dolore magna aliqua. Ut enim ad minim veniam, quis nostrud exercitation ullamco laboris nisi ut aliquip ex ea commodo consequat.

Duis aute irure dolor in reprehenderit in voluptate velit esse cillum dolore eu fugiat nulla pariatur. Excepteur sint occaecat cupidatat non proident, sunt in culpa qui officia deserunt mollit anim id est laborum.

Birthdays

Lorem ipsum dolor sit amet, consectetur adipisicing elit, sed do eiusmod tempor incididunt ut labore et dolore magna aliqua. Ut enim ad minim veniam, quis nostrud exercitation ullamco laboris nisi ut aliquip ex ea commodo consequat.

Duis aute irure dolor in reprehenderit in voluptate velit esse cillum dolore eu fugiat nulla pariatur. Excepteur sint occaecat cupidatat non proident, sunt in culpa qui officia deserunt mollit anim id est laborum.

Being Awesome

"Lorem ipsum dolor sit amet, consectetur adipisicing elit, sed do eiusmod tempor incididunt ut labore et dolore magna aliqua. Ut enim ad minim veniam."

Send newsworthy things to news@awesomeco.com.

Figure 9—Our single-column newsletter is harder to read because it's very wide.

markup elements like section and such for this newsletter, it's because our fallback method isn't compatible with those elements in Internet Explorer.

```
css3columns/condensed_newsletter.html
<body>
  <div id="header">
    <h1>AwesomeCo Newsletter</h1>
    <p>Volume 3, Issue 12</p>
  </div>

  <div id="newsletter">
    <div id="director_news">
      <div>
        <h2>News From The Director</h2>
      </div>
      <div>
        <p>
          Lorem ipsum dolor...
        </p>
        <div class="callout">
          <h4>Being Awesome</h4>
          <p>
            &quot;Lorem ipsum dolor sit amet...&quot;
          </p>
        </div>
      </div>
```

```
      <p>
        Duis aute irure...
      </p>
    </div>
  </div>

  <div id="awesome_bits">
    <div>
      <h2>Quick Bits of Awesome</h2>
    </div>
    <div>
      <p>
        Lorem ipsum...
      </p>
      <p>
        Duis aute irure...
      </p>
    </div>
  </div>

  <div id="birthdays">
    <div>
      <h2>Birthdays</h2>
    </div>
    <div>
      <p>
        Lorem ipsum dolor...
      </p>
      <p>
        Duis aute irure...
      </p>
    </div>
  </div>

</div>
<div id="footer">
  <h6>Send newsworthy things to
    <a href="mailto:news@aweseomco.com">news@awesomeco.com</a>.
  </h6>
</div>
</body>
```

To split this into a two-column layout, all we need to do is add this to our style sheet:

```
css3columns/newsletter.html
#newsletter{
  column-count: 2;
  -moz-column-count: 2;
  -webkit-column-count: 2;
  -moz-column-gap: 20px;
```

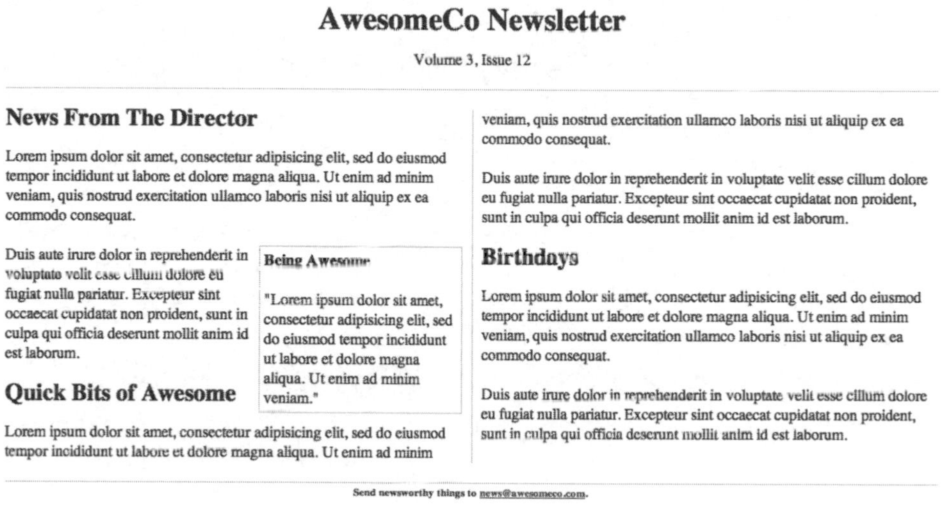

AwesomeCo Newsletter

Volume 3, Issue 12

News From The Director

Lorem ipsum dolor sit amet, consectetur adipisicing elit, sed do eiusmod tempor incididunt ut labore et dolore magna aliqua. Ut enim ad minim veniam, quis nostrud exercitation ullamco laboris nisi ut aliquip ex ea commodo consequat.

Duis aute irure dolor in reprehenderit in voluptate velit esse cillum dolore eu fugiat nulla pariatur. Excepteur sint occaecat cupidatat non proident, sunt in culpa qui officia deserunt mollit anim id est laborum.

Quick Bits of Awesome

Lorem ipsum dolor sit amet, consectetur adipisicing elit, sed do eiusmod tempor incididunt ut labore et dolore magna aliqua. Ut enim ad minim

Being Awesome

"Lorem ipsum dolor sit amet, consectetur adipisicing elit, sed do eiusmod tempor incididunt ut labore et dolore magna aliqua. Ut enim ad minim veniam."

veniam, quis nostrud exercitation ullamco laboris nisi ut aliquip ex ea commodo consequat.

Duis aute irure dolor in reprehenderit in voluptate velit esse cillum dolore eu fugiat nulla pariatur. Excepteur sint occaecat cupidatat non proident, sunt in culpa qui officia deserunt mollit anim id est laborum.

Birthdays

Lorem ipsum dolor sit amet, consectetur adipisicing elit, sed do eiusmod tempor incididunt ut labore et dolore magna aliqua. Ut enim ad minim veniam, quis nostrud exercitation ullamco laboris nisi ut aliquip ex ea commodo consequat.

Duis aute irure dolor in reprehenderit in voluptate velit esse cillum dolore eu fugiat nulla pariatur. Excepteur sint occaecat cupidatat non proident, sunt in culpa qui officia deserunt mollit anim id est laborum.

Send newsworthy things to news@awesomeco.com.

Figure 10—Our new two-column newsletter

```
  column-gap: 20px;
  -webkit-column-gap: 20px;
  -moz-column-rule: 1px solid #ddccb5;
  -webkit-column-rule: 1px solid #ddccb5;
  column-rule: 1px solid #ddccb5;
}
```

Now we have something much nicer, like you see in Figure 10, *Our new two-column newsletter*, on page 73. We can add more content, and the browser will automatically determine how to split the content evenly. Also, notice that the floated elements float to the columns that contain them.

Falling Back

CSS3 columns don't work in Internet Explorer 9 and older, so we'll use the jQuery Columnizer plug-in[5] as a fallback. Columnizer will let us split our content evenly by simply using code like this:

css3columns/newsletter.html
```
$("#newsletter").columnize({ columns: 2 });
```

People without JavaScript are going to be stuck with a single column of text, but they'll still be able to read the content, because we marked it up in a linear fashion, so we have them covered. However, we can use JavaScript to detect

---

5.   http://welcome.totheinter.net/columnizer-jquery-plugin/

> **Joe asks:**
> # Can I Specify Different Widths for Each Column?
>
> Nope. Your columns must each be the same size. I was a little surprised too at first, so I double-checked the specification, and at the time of writing, there was no provision for specifying multiple column widths.
>
> However, when you think about how columns are traditionally used, it makes sense. Columns are not meant to be a hack to easily make a sidebar for your website any more than tables are. Columns are meant to make reading long areas of text easier, and equal width columns are perfect for that.

browser support for certain elements. If we retrieve a CSS property that exists, we'll get an empty string. If we get a null value back, we don't have that property available.

css3columns/newsletter.html

```
<script
  charset="utf-8"
  src='http://ajax.googleapis.com/ajax/libs/jquery/1.4.2/jquery.min.js'
  type='text/javascript'>
</script>

<script
  charset="utf-8"
  src="javascripts/autocolumn.js"
  type='text/javascript'>
</script>

<script type="text/javascript">
  function hasColumnSupport(){
    var element = document.documentElement;
    var style = element.style;
    if (style){
      return typeof style.columnCount == "string" ||
        typeof style.MozColumnCount == "string" ||
        typeof style.WebkitColumnCount == "string" ||
        typeof style.KhtmlColumnCount == "string";
    }
    return null;
  }

  $(function(){
    if(!hasColumnSupport()){
     $("#newsletter").columnize({ columns: 2 });
    }
  });
</script>
```

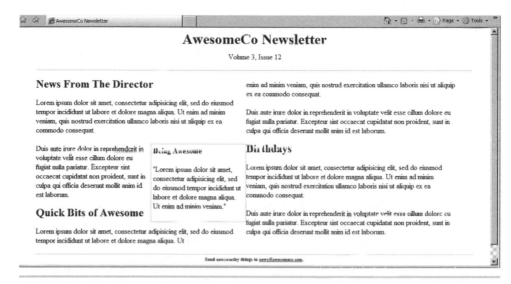

Figure 11—Our Internet Explorer version works but needs some minor adjustments.

We simply check for column support, and if none exists, we apply our plug-in.

Refresh the page in Internet Explorer, and you'll now see your two-column newsletter. It may not be perfect, as you can see in Figure 11, *Our Internet Explorer version works but needs some minor adjustments.*, on page 75, so you'll need to use a little CSS or JavaScript to fix any elements that don't quite look right, but I'm leaving that exercise up to you. Take advantage of conditional comments like we used in *Use JavaScript*, on page 63 to target specific versions of Internet Explorer if needed.

Separating your content into multiple columns can make your content easier to read. However, if your page is longer, your users might find it annoying to have to scroll back to the top to read the columns. Use this with care.

Tip 10

Building Mobile Interfaces with Media Queries

We've been able to define media-specific style sheets for quite a while, but we've been limited to the type of output, as you saw in Tip 8, *Making Links Printable with :after and content*, on page 66, when we defined our print style sheet. CSS3's media queries[6] let us change the presentation of a page based on the screen size our visitors use. Web developers have done screen size detection for years using JavaScript to obtain information about the user's screen size. But we can start to do that with style sheets alone. We can use media queries to determine the following:

- Resolution
- Orientation (portrait or landscape mode)
- Device width and height
- Width and height of the browser window

Because of this, media queries make it very easy for us to create alternative style sheets for mobile users.

It turns out that the AwesomeCo executive staff have all just dumped their BlackBerry devices for shiny new iPhones. The marketing director would love to see an iPhone-ready version of the blog template we built in Tip 1, *Redefining a Blog Using Semantic Markup*, on page 14. We can do that very quickly.

Our current blog is a two-column layout, with a main content region and a sidebar. The easiest way to make this more readable on the iPhone is to remove the floating elements so that the sidebar falls beneath the main content. That way, the reader won't have to scroll sideways on the device.

To make this work, we'll add this code to the bottom of the blog's style sheet:

```
css3mediaquery/style.css
@media only screen and (max-device-width: 480px) {
  body{
    width:460px;
  }
```

---

6.   http://www.w3.org/TR/css3-mediaqueries/

> ### Joe asks:
> ## What About the Handheld Media Type?
>
> The Handheld media type was designed to let us target mobile devices like we target printers, but most mobile devices want to show you the "real Internet" and so they ignore that media type, serving the style sheet associated with the screen media type instead.

```
section#sidebar, section#posts{
  float: none;
  width: 100%;
  }
}
```

You can think of the code we put within the media query braces as its own style sheet, invoked when the conditions of the query are met. In this case, we resize the body of the page and turn our two-column layout into a single-column layout.

We could also use media queries when we link the style sheet, so we can keep our mobile style sheet in a separate file, like this:

```
<link rel="stylesheet" type="text/css"
  href="CSS/mobile.css" media="only screen and (max-device-width: 480px)">
```

With that, our blog immediately becomes more readable on the iPhone. You can use this approach to build style sheets for other displays as well, such as kiosks, tablets, and displays of various sizes so that your content is readable in more places.

Falling Back

Media queries are supported in Firefox, Chrome, Safari, Opera, and Internet Explorer 9. You'll have to rely on JavaScript fallback solutions to load additional style sheets based on the user's device. Our example targets iPhones, so we don't need a fallback solution—our content is readable without the media query.

However, if you want to experiment with media queries in other browsers, there is a jQuery plug-in[7] that adds basic media query support to other browsers. It's limited in that it works only with linked style sheets, and it only supports min-width and max-width in pixels. Even with those limitations, it works very well for creating different interfaces for different window sizes.

---

7. http://www.protofunc.com/scripts/jquery/mediaqueries

4.1 The Future

The things we talked about in this chapter improve the user interface, but people can still work with our products if their browsers don't support these new features. People can still read the data in the table if it's not styled with stripes; the forms will still work, even if they don't have rounded corners on the interface elements; and the newsletter won't be laid out in multiple columns. It's good to know that we can use the presentation layer to achieve these effects instead of having to resort to JavaScript or server-side solutions.

Almost all browsers support these selectors now, with the exception of Internet Explorer. As we move forward, you can expect to see IE moving to support these as well, especially the pseudoclasses. When the specification becomes final, the vendor-specific prefixes like moz and webkit- go away. Once that happens, you'll be able to remove your fallback code.

CHAPTER 5

Improving Accessibility

Many of the new elements in HTML5 help you more accurately describe your content. This becomes more important when other programs start interpreting your code. For example, some people use software called *screen readers* to translate the graphical contents of the screen to text that's read aloud. Screen readers work by interpreting the text on the screen and the corresponding markup to identify links, images, and other elements. Screen readers have made amazing advances, but they are always lagging behind the current trends. Live regions on pages, where polling or Ajax requests alter content on the page, are difficult to detect. More complex pages can be difficult to navigate because of the screen reader needing to read a lot of the content aloud.

Accessibility for Rich Internet Applications (WIA-ARIA)[1] is a specification that provides ways to improve the accessibility of websites, especially web applications. It is especially useful if you are developing applications with JavaScript controls and Ajax. Some parts of the WIA-ARIA specification have been rolled into HTML5, while others remain separate and can complement the HTML5 specification. Many screen readers are already using features of the WIA_ARIA specification, including JAWS, WindowEyes, and even Apple's built-in VoiceOver feature. WIA-ARIA also introduces additional markup that assistive technology can use as hints for discovering regions that are updatable.

In this chapter, we'll see how HTML5 can improve the experience of your visitors who use these assistive devices. Most importantly, the techniques in this chapter require no fallback support, because many screen readers are already able to take advantage of these techniques right now.

---

1. http://www.w3.org/WAI/intro/aria.php

These techniques include:[2]

The role attribute [<div role="document">]
> Identifies responsibility of an element to screen readers. *[C3, F3.6, S4, IE8, O9.6]*

aria-live [<div aria-live="polite">]
> Identifies a region that updates automatically, possibly by Ajax. *[F3.6 (Windows), S4, IE8]*

aria-atomic [<div aria-live="polite" aria-atomic="true">]
> Identifies whether the entire content of a live region should be read or just the elements that changed. *[F3.6 (Windows), S4, IE8]*

---

2. In the descriptions that follow, browser support is shown in square brackets using a shorthand code and the minimum supported version number. The codes used are *C:* Google Chrome, *F:* Firefox, *IE:* Internet Explorer, *O:* Opera, *S:* Safari, *IOS:* iOS devices with Mobile Safari, and *A:* Android Browser.

Tip 11

Providing Navigation Hints with ARIA Roles

Most websites share a common structure: there's a header, a navigation section, some main content, and a footer. Most of these sites are coded just like that, in a linear fashion. Unfortunately, this means that a screen reader may have to read the site to its user in that order. Since most sites repeat the same header and navigation on each page, the user will have to hear these elements each time they visit another page.

The recommended fix is to provide a hidden "skip navigation" link that screen readers will read aloud, which simply links to an anchor somewhere near the main content. However, that's not something that's built in, and it's not something that everyone knows how (or remembers) to do.

HTML5's new role attribute lets us assign a "responsibility" to each element on your page. A screen reader can then very easily parse the page and categorize all of those responsibilities so that you can create a simple index for the page. For example, it can find all the navigation roles on the page and present them to the user so they can quickly navigate around your application.

These roles come from the WIA-ARIA specification[3] and have been incorporated into the HTML5 specification. There are two specific classifications of roles that you can put to use right now: landmark roles and document roles.

Landmark Roles

Landmark roles identify "points of interest" on your site, such as the banner, search area, or navigation that screen readers can quickly identify.

Role	Use
banner	Identifies the banner area of your page
search	Identifies the search area of your page
navigation	Identifies navigational elements on your page
main	Identifies where your page's main content begins

---

3. http://www.w3.org/WAI/PF/aria/roles

Role	Use
contentinfo	Identifies where information about the content exists, such as copyright information and publication date
complementary	Identifies content on a page that complements the main content but is meaningful on its own
application	Identifies a region of a page that contains a web application as opposed to a web document

We can apply a few of these roles to the AwesomeCo blog template we worked on in Tip 1, *Redefining a Blog Using Semantic Markup*, on page 14.

For the overall header, let's apply the banner role like this:

```
html5_aria/blog/index.html
<header id="page_header" role="banner">
  <h1>AwesomeCo Blog!</h1>
</header>
```

All that's needed is the addition of the role="banner" to the existing header tag.

We can identify our navigation the same way:

```
html5_aria/blog/index.html
<nav role="navigation">
  <ul>
    <li><a href="/">Latest Posts</a></li>
    <li><a href="/archives">Archives</a></li>
    <li><a href="/contributors">Contributors</a></li>
    <li><a href="/contact">Contact Us</a></li>
  </ul>
</nav>
```

The HTML5 specification says that some elements have default roles and can't be overridden. The nav element must have the role of navigation and technically doesn't need to be specified. Screen readers aren't quite ready to accept that default yet, but many of them do understand these ARIA roles.

Our main and sidebar regions can be identified as follows:

```
html5_aria/blog/index.html
<section id="posts" role="main">
</section>
```

```
html5_aria/blog/index.html
<section id="sidebar" role="complementary">
  <nav>
    <h3>Archives</h3>
    <ul>
      <li><a href="2010/10">October 2010</a></li>
```

```
    <li><a href="2010/09">September 2010</a></li>
    <li><a href="2010/08">August 2010</a></li>
    <li><a href="2010/07">July 2010</a></li>
    <li><a href="2010/06">June 2010</a></li>
    <li><a href="2010/05">May 2010</a></li>
    <li><a href="2010/04">April 2010</a></li>
    <li><a href="2010/03">March 2010</a></li>
    <li><a href="2010/02">February 2010</a></li>
    <li><a href="2010/01">January 2010</a></li>
  </ul>
 </nav>
</section> <!-- sidebar -->
```

We identify the publication and copyright info in our footer using the contentinfo role like this:

html5_aria/blog/index.html

```
<footer id="page_footer" role="contentinfo">
  <p>&copy; 2010 AwesomeCo.</p>
</footer> <!-- footer -->
```

If we had a search for our blog, we could identify that region as well. Now that we've identified the landmarks, let's take this a step further and help identify some of the document elements.

Document Structure Roles

Document structure roles help screen readers identify parts of static content easily, which can help better organize content for navigation.

Role	Use
document	Identifies a region containing document content, as opposed to application content.
article	Identifies a composition that forms an independent part of a document.
definition	Identifies a definition of a term or subject.
directory	Identifies a list of references to a group, like a table of contents. Used for static content.
heading	Identifies a heading for a section of a page.
img	Identifies a section that contains elements of an image. This may be image elements as well as captions and descriptive text.
list	Identifies a group of noninteractive list items.

Role	Use
listitem	Identifies a single member of a group of noninteractive list items.
math	Identifies a mathematical expression.
note	Identifies content that is parenthetic or ancillary to the main content of the resource.
presentation	Identifies content that is for presentation and can be ignored by assistive technology.
row	Identifies a row of cells in a grid.
rowheader	Identifies a cell containing header information for a row in a grid.

Many of the document roles are implicitly defined by HTML tags, such as articles and headers. However, the document role isn't, and it's a very helpful role, especially in applications with a mix of dynamic and static content. For example, a web-based email client may have the document role attached to the element that contains the body of the email message. This is useful because screen readers often have different methods for navigating using the keyboard. When the screen reader's focus is on an application element, it may need to allow keypresses through to the web application. However, when the focus is on static content, it could allow the screen reader's key bindings to work differently.

We can apply the document role to our blog by adding it to the body element.

html5_aria/blog/index.html

```
<body role="document">
```

This can help ensure that a screen reader will treat this page as static content.

Falling Back

These roles are already usable on the latest browsers with the latest screen readers, so you can start working with them now. Browsers that don't support them are just going to ignore them, so you're really only helping those people who can use them.

Joe asks:
Do We Need These Landmark Roles If We Have Elements Such As nav and header?

The landmark roles may at first seem redundant, but they provide you with the flexibility you need for situations where you can't use the new elements.

Using the search role, you can direct your users to the region of the page that not only contains the search field but also links to a site map, a drop-down list of "quick links," or other elements that will help your users find information quickly, as opposed to just directing them to the actual search field.

There are also a lot more roles introduced by the specification than there are new elements and form controls.

Tip 12

Creating an Accessible Updatable Region

We do a lot of things with Ajax in our web applications these days. Standard practice is to fire off some sort of visual effect to give the user a clue that something has changed on the page. However, a person using a screen reader obviously isn't going to be able to see any visual cues. The WIA-ARIA specification provides a pretty nice alternative solution that currently works in IE, Firefox, and Safari with various popular screen readers.

The AwesomeCo executive director of communications wants a new home page. It should have links to a "services" section, a "contact" section, and an "about" section. He insists that the home page shouldn't scroll because "people hate scrolling." He would like you to implement a prototype for the page with a horizontal menu that changes the page's main content when clicked. That's easy enough to implement, and with the aria-live attribute, we can do something we haven't been able to do well before—implement this type of interface in a way that's friendly to screen readers.

Let's build a simple interface like Figure 12, *A mock-up of the home page using jQuery to change the main content*, on page 87. We'll put all the content on the home page, and if JavaScript is available to us, we'll hide all but the first entry. We'll make the navigation links point to each section using page anchors, and we'll use jQuery to change those anchor links into events that swap out the main content. People with JavaScript will see what our director wants, and people without will still be able to see all the content on the page.

Creating the Page

We'll start by creating a basic HTML5 page, and we'll add our Welcome section, which will be the default section displayed to users when they visit the page. Here's the code for the page with the navigation bar and the jump links:

```
html5_aria/homepage/index.html
<!DOCTYPE html>
<html lang="en-US">
  <head>
    <meta http-equiv="Content-Type" content="text/html; charset=utf-8">
    <title>AwesomeCo</title>
    <link rel="stylesheet" href="style.css" type="text/css">
```

AwesomeCo

Welcome   Services   Contact   About

Welcome

The welcome section

© 2010 AwesomeCo.

Home   About   Terms of Service   Privacy

Figure 12—A mock-up of the home page using jQuery to change the main content

```html
</head>
<body>
  <header id="header">
    <h1>AwesomeCo </h1>
    <nav>
      <ul>
        <li><a href="#welcome">Welcome</a></li>
        <li><a href="#services">Services</a></li>
        <li><a href="#contact">Contact</a></li>
        <li><a href="#about">About</a></li>
      </ul>
    </nav>
  </header>
  <section id="content"
           role="document" aria-live="assertive" aria-atomic="true">

    <section id="welcome">
      <header>
        <h2>Welcome</h2>
      </header>
      <p>The welcome section</p>
    </section>
  </section>
  <footer id="footer">
    <p>&copy; 2010 AwesomeCo.</p>
    <nav>
      <ul>
        <li><a href="http://awesomeco.com/">Home</a></li>
        <li><a href="about">About</a></li>
        <li><a href="terms.html">Terms of Service</a></li>
        <li><a href="privacy.html">Privacy</a></li>
      </ul>
    </nav>
  </footer>
</body>
</html>
```

The Welcome section has an ID of welcome, which matches the anchor in the navigation bar. We can declare our additional page sections in the same fashion.

html5_aria/homepage/index.html

```
<section id="services">
  <header>
    <h2>Services</h2>
  </header>
  <p>The services section</p>
</section>

<section id="contact">
  <header>
    <h2>Contact</h2>
  </header>
  <p>The contact section</p>
</section>

<section id="about">
  <header>
    <h2>About</h2>
  </header>
  <p>The about section</p>
</section>
```

Our four content regions are wrapped by this markup:

html5_aria/homepage/index.html

```
<section id="content"
         role="document" aria-live="assertive" aria-atomic="true">
```

The attributes on this line tell screen readers that this region of the page updates.

Polite and Assertive Updating

There are two types of methods for alerting the user to changes on the page when using aria-live. The polite method is designed to not interrupt the user's workflow. For example, if the user's screen reader is reading a sentence and another region of the page updates and the mode is set to polite, then the screen reader will finish reading the current sentence. However, if the mode was set to assertive, then it's considered high priority, and the screen reader will stop and begin reading the new content. It's really important that you use the appropriate type of interruption when you're developing your site. Overuse of "assertive" can disorient and confuse your users. Only use assertive if you absolutely must. In our case, it's the right choice, because we will be hiding the other content.

Atomic Updating

The second parameter, aria-atomic=true, instructs the screen reader to read the entire contents of the changed region. If we set it to false, it would tell the screen reader to only read nodes that changed. We're replacing the entire content, so telling the screen reader to read it all makes sense in this case. If we were replacing a single list item or appending to a table with Ajax, we would want to use false instead.

Hiding Regions

To hide the regions, we need to write a little bit of JavaScript and attach it to our page. We'll create a file called application.js, and then we include this file as well as the jQuery library on our page.

`html5_aria/homepage/index.html`

```html
<script type="text/javascript"
    charset="utf-8"
    src="http://ajax.googleapis.com/ajax/libs/jquery/1.4.2/jquery.min.js">
</script>

<script type="text/javascript"
    charset="utf-8"
    src="javascripts/application.js">
</script>
```

Our application.js file contains this simple script:

`html5_aria/homepage/javascripts/application.js`

```javascript
// HTML5 structural element support for IE 6, 7, and 8
document.createElement("header");
document.createElement("footer");
document.createElement("section");
document.createElement("aside");
document.createElement("article");
document.createElement("nav");

$(function(){

  $("#services, #about, #contact").hide().addClass("hidden");
  $("#welcome").addClass("visible");

  $("nav ul").click(function(event){

    target = $(event.target);
    if(target.is("a")){
      event.preventDefault();
      if ( $(target.attr("href")).hasClass("hidden") ){
        $(".visible").removeClass("visible")
          .addClass("hidden")
```

```
                  .hide();
              $(target.attr("href"))
                  .removeClass("hidden")
25                .addClass("visible")
                  .show();
            };
         };

30    });

    });
```

On line 11, we hide the "services," "about," and "contact" sections. We also apply a class of "hidden" to them, and then on the next line we apply a class of "visible" to the default "welcome" section. Adding these classes makes it really easy to identify which sections need to be turned off and on when we do the toggle.

We capture any clicks to the navigation bar on line 14, and then we determine which element was clicked on 17. If the user clicked a link, we check to see whether the corresponding section is hidden. The href attribute of the clicked link can easily help us locate the corresponding section using jQuery selectors, which you can see on line 19.

If it's hidden, we hide everything else and then show the selected section. That's all there is to it. The screen readers should detect the region changes.

Falling Back

Like roles, this solution can be used right now by the latest versions of screen readers. By following good practices such as unobtrusive JavaScript, we have a simple implementation that can work for a reasonably wide audience. Older browsers and screen readers will ignore the additional attributes, so there's no danger in adding them to our markup.

5.1   The Future

HTML5 and the WIA-ARIA specification have paved the way for a much more accessible Web. With the ability to identify changing regions on the page, developers can develop richer JavaScript applications without worrying so much about accessibility issues.

Part II

New Sights and Sounds

CHAPTER 6

Drawing on the Canvas

In the second part of this book, we'll shift from talking about structure and interfaces to looking at how we can use HTML5 and CSS3 to draw, work with multimedia files, and create our own interface elements. We'll start off by spending some time making some graphics using HTML5's new canvas element.

If you wanted an image in a web application, you'd traditionally open your graphics software of choice, create an image, and embed it on your page with an img tag. If you wanted animations, you'd use Flash. HTML5's canvas element lets developers create images and animations in the browser programmatically using JavaScript. We can use the canvas to create simple or complex shapes or even create graphs and charts without resorting to server-side libraries, Flash, or other plug-ins. Coincidentally, we'll do both of these things in this chapter.[1]

<canvas> [<canvas><p>Alternative content</p></canvas>]

> Supports creation of vector-based graphics via JavaScript. *[C4, F3, IE9, S3.2, O10.1, IOS3.2, A2]*

First we'll get familiar with how we use JavaScript and the canvas element together by drawing some simple shapes as we construct a version of the AwesomeCo logo. Then we'll use a graphing library that's specifically designed to work with the canvas to create a bar graph of browser statistics. We'll also discuss some of the special fallback challenges that we'll face because the canvas is more of a programming interface than an element.

---

1. In the description that follows, browser support is shown in square brackets. The codes used are *C:* Google Chrome, *F:* Firefox, *IE:* Internet Explorer, *O:* Opera, *S:* Safari, *IOS:* iOS devices with Mobile Safari, and *A:* Android Browser.

Tip 13

Drawing a Logo

The canvas element is a container element much like the script element. It's a blank slate we can draw on. We define a canvas with a width and height like this:

html5canvasgraph/canvas_simple_drawing.html
```
<canvas id="my_canvas" width="150" height="150">
  Fallback content here
</canvas>
```

Unfortunately, you can't use CSS to control or alter the width and height of a canvas element without distorting the contents, so you need to decide on your canvas dimensions when you declare it.

We use JavaScript to put shapes on the canvas. Even if you provided fallback content to those browsers without the canvas element, you still need to prevent the JavaScript code from trying to manipulate it. Find the canvas by its ID, and see whether the browser supports the canvas' getContext method.

html5canvasgraph/canvas_simple_drawing.html
```
var canvas = document.getElementById('my_canvas');
if (canvas.getContext){
  var context = canvas.getContext('2d');

}else{
  // do something to show the canvas' hidden contents
  // or let the browser display the text within the <canvas> element.
}
```

If we get a response from the getContext method, we grab the 2D context for the canvas so we can add objects. If we don't have a context, we need to devise a way to display the fallback content. Since we know that the canvas element requires JavaScript in order to work, we're building a framework to handle fallbacks from the beginning.

Once you have the canvas' context, you simply add elements to that context. To add a red box, you set the fill color and then create the box, like this:

html5canvasgraph/canvas_simple_drawing.html
```
context.fillStyle = "rgb(200,0,0)";
context.fillRect (10, 10, 100, 100);
```

The canvas's 2D context is a grid, with the top-left corner as the default origin. When you create a shape, you specify the starting X and Y coordinates and the width and height.

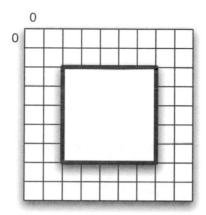

Each shape is added onto its own layer, so you could create three boxes with a 10-pixel offset, like this:

html5canvasgraph/canvas_simple_drawing.html
```
context.fillStyle = "rgb(200,0,0)";
context.fillRect (10, 10, 100, 100);
context.fillStyle = "rgb(0,200,0)";
context.fillRect (20, 20, 100, 100);

context.fillStyle = "rgb(0,0,200)";
context.fillRect (30, 30, 100, 100);
```

and they'll stack on top of each other, like this:

Now that you have an understanding of the basics of drawing, let's put together the AwesomeCo logo. It's pretty simple, as you can see from Figure 13, *The AwesomeCo logo*, on page 96.

Figure 13—The AwesomeCo logo

Drawing the Logo

The logo consists of a string of text, an angled path, a square, and a triangle. Let's start by creating a new HTML5 document, adding a canvas element to the page, and then creating a JavaScript function for drawing the logo, which detects whether we can use the 2D canvas.

html5canvasgraph/logo.html
```
var drawLogo = function(){
  var canvas = document.getElementById('logo');
  var context = canvas.getContext('2d');
};
```

We invoke this method after first checking for the existence of the canvas element, like this:

html5canvasgraph/logo.html
```
$(function(){
  var canvas = document.getElementById('logo');
  if (canvas.getContext){
    drawLogo();
  }
});
```

Notice here we're using the jQuery function again to ensure that the event fires when the document is ready. We're looking for an element on the page with the ID of logo, so we'd better make sure we add our canvas element to the document so it can be found, and our detection will work.

html5canvasgraph/logo.html
```
<canvas id="logo" width="900" height="80">
  <h1>AwesomeCo</h1>
</canvas>
```

Next, let's add the "AwesomeCo" text to the canvas.

Adding Text

Adding text to the canvas involves choosing a font, a font size, and an alignment, and then applying the text to the appropriate coordinates on the grid. We can add the text "AwesomeCo" to our canvas like this:

```
html5canvasgraph/logo.html
context.font = 'italic 40px sans-serif';
context.textBaseline = 'top';
context.fillText('AwesomeCo', 60, 0);
```

We're defining the text type and setting its baseline, or vertical alignment, before we apply it to the canvas. We're using the fillText method so we get text that's filled in with the fill color, and we're setting it 60 pixels to the right so we can make room for the large triangle-shaped path we'll draw next.

Drawing Lines

We draw lines on the canvas by playing a game of "connect-the-dots." We specify a starting point on the canvas grid and then specify additional points on the grid to move to. As we move around the canvas, the dots get connected, like this:

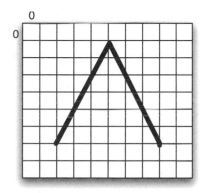

We use the beginPath() method to start drawing a line, and then we create our path, like this:

```
html5canvasgraph/logo.html
context.lineWidth = 2;
context.beginPath();
context.moveTo(0, 40);
context.lineTo(30, 0);
context.lineTo(60, 40 );
context.lineTo(285, 40 );
context.stroke();
context.closePath();
```

When we're all done moving around the canvas, we have to call the stroke method to draw the line and then call the closePath method to stop drawing.

Now all that's left is the box and triangle combination that sits within the big triangle.

Moving the Origin

We need to draw a small square and triangle inside the larger triangle. When we draw shapes and paths, we can specify the X and Y coordinates from the origin at the top-left corner of the canvas, but we can also just move the origin to a new location.

Let's draw the smaller inner square by moving the origin.

html5canvasgraph/logo.html
```
context.save();
context.translate(20,20);
context.fillRect(0,0,20,20);
```

Notice that before we move the origin, we call the save() method. This saves the previous state of the canvas so we can revert easily. It's like a restore point, and you can think of it as a stack. Every time you call save(), you get a new entry. When we're all done, we'll call restore(), which will restore the top savepoint on the stack.

Now let's use paths to draw the inner triangle, but instead of using a stroke, we'll use a fill to create the illusion that the triangle is "cutting into" the square.

html5canvasgraph/logo.html
```
context.fillStyle    = '#fff';
context.strokeStyle = '#fff';

context.lineWidth = 2;
context.beginPath();
context.moveTo(0, 20);
context.lineTo(10, 0);
context.lineTo(20, 20 );
context.lineTo(0, 20 );
context.fill();
context.closePath();
context.restore();
```

Here we set the stroke and fill to white (#fff) before we begin drawing. Then we draw our lines, and since we moved the origin previously, we're relative to the top-left corner of the square we just drew.

We're almost done, but it needs a little color.

Adding Colors

In *Moving the Origin*, on page 98, you saw briefly how to set the stroke and fill color for the drawing tools. We could set the color of everything to red just by adding this code before we draw anything:

html5canvasgraph/logo.html

```
context.fillStyle = "#f00";
context.strokeStyle = "#f00";
```

But that's a little boring. We can create gradients and assign those to strokes and fills like this:

html5canvasgraph/logo_gradient.html

```
// context.fillStyle = "#f00";
// context.strokeStyle = "#f00";
var gradient = context.createLinearGradient(0, 0, 0, 40);
gradient.addColorStop(0,   '#a00'); // red
gradient.addColorStop(1,   '#f00'); // red
context.fillStyle = gradient;
context.strokeStyle = gradient;
```

We just create a gradient object and set the color stops of the gradient. In this example, we're just going between two shades of red, but we could do a rainbow if we wanted.[2]

Note that we have to set the color of things before we draw them.

At this point, our logo is complete, and we have a better understanding of how we draw simple shapes on the canvas. However, versions of Internet Explorer prior to IE9 don't have any support for the canvas element. Let's fix that.

Falling Back

Google released a library called ExplorerCanvas[3] that makes most of the Canvas API available to Internet Explorer users. All we have to do is include this library on our page:

html5canvasgraph/logo_gradient.html

```
<!--[if lte IE 8]>
<script src="javascripts/excanvas.js"></script>
<![endif]-->
```

and things should work just fine in Internet Explorer—but they don't work just yet. At the time of writing, the most stable release doesn't support adding text at all, and the version from the Subversion repository[4] doesn't use the correct fonts. Also, there's no support yet for adding gradients on strokes with this library.

---

2. Do *not* do a rainbow, please!
3. http://code.google.com/p/explorercanvas/
4. http://explorercanvas.googlecode.com/svn/trunk/excanvas.js

So, instead, we rely on other solutions, such as placing a PNG of the logo inside the canvas element, or we simply don't use the canvas at all. Since this was just an exercise to show you how to draw, it's not the end of the world if we can't use this particular example in a cross-platform production system yet.

Tip 14

Graphing Statistics with RGraph

AwesomeCo is doing a lot of work on the website, and senior management would like to see a graph of the web stats. The back-end programmers will be able to get the data in real time, but first they'd like to see whether you can come up with a way to display the graph in the browser, so they've provided you with some test data. Our goal is to transform that test data into something that resembles Figure 14, *A client-side bar graph using the canvas*, on page 102.

There are lots of ways to draw graphs on a web page. Developers use Flash for graphs all the time, but that has the limitation of not working on some mobile devices like the iPad or iPhone. There are server-side solutions that work well, but those might be too processor-intensive if you're working with real-time data. A standards-based client-side solution like the canvas is a great option as long as we're careful to ensure it works in older browsers. You've already seen how to draw squares, but drawing something complex requires a lot more JavaScript. We need a graphing library to help us along.

The fact that HTML5 isn't available everywhere yet hasn't stopped the developers of the RGraph library.[5] RGraph makes it ridiculously simple to draw graphs using the HTML5 canvas. It's a pure JavaScript solution, though, so it won't work for those user agents that don't have JavaScript available, but then again, neither will the canvas. Here's the code for a very simple bar graph:

```
html5canvasgraph/rgraph_bar_example.html
<canvas width="500" height="250" id="test">[no canvas support]</canvas>

<script type="text/javascript" charset="utf-8">
  var bar = new RGraph.Bar('test', [50,25,15,10]);
  bar.Set('chart.gutter', 50);
  bar.Set('chart.colors', ['red']);
  bar.Set('chart.title', "A bar graph of my favorite pies");
  bar.Set('chart.labels', ["Banana Creme", "Pumpkin", "Apple", "Cherry"]);
  bar.Draw();
</script>
```

---

5. http://www.rgraph.net/

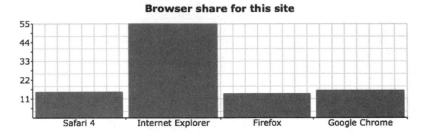

Figure 14—A client-side bar graph using the canvas

All we have to do is create a couple of JavaScript arrays, and the library draws the graph on the canvas for us.

Describing Data with HTML

We could hard-code the values for the browser statistics in the JavaScript code, but then only users with JavaScript would be able to see the values. Instead, let's put the data right on the page as text. We can read the data with JavaScript and feed it to the graphing library later.

```
html5canvasgraph/canvas_graph.html
<div id="graph_data">
  <h1>Browser share for this site</h1>
  <ul>
    <li>
      <p data-name="Safari 4" data-percent="15">
        Safari 4 - 15%
      </p>
    </li>
    <li>
      <p data-name="Internet Explorer" data-percent="55">
        Internet Explorer - 55%
      </p>
    </li>
    <li>
      <p data-name="Firefox" data-percent="14">
        Firefox - 14%
      </p>
    </li>
    <li>
      <p data-name="Google Chrome" data-percent="16">
        Google Chrome - 16%
      </p>
    </li>
  </ul>
</div>
```

We're using the HTML5 data attributes to store the browser names and the percentages. Although we have that information in the text, it's so much easier to work with programmatically since we won't have to parse strings.

If you open up the page in your browser or just look at Figure 15, *Our graph as HTML*, on page 104, you'll see that the graph data is nicely displayed and readable even without the graph. This will be your fallback content for mobile devices and other users where either the canvas element or JavaScript is not available.

Now, let's turn this markup into a graph.

Turning Our HTML into a Bar Graph

We're going to use a bar graph, so we'll need to require both the RGraph Bar graph library as well as the main RGraph library. We'll also use jQuery to grab the data out of the document. In the head section of the HTML page, we need to load the libraries we need.

```
html5canvasgraph/canvas_graph.html
<script type="text/javascript"
  charset="utf-8"
  src="http://ajax.googleapis.com/ajax/libs/jquery/1.4.2/jquery.min.js">
</script>
<script src="javascripts/RGraph.common.js" ></script>
<script src="javascripts/RGraph.bar.js" ></script>
```

To build the graph, we need to grab the graph's title, the labels, and the data from the HTML document and pass it to the RGraph library. RGraph takes in arrays for both the labels and the data. We can use jQuery to quickly build those arrays.

```
html5canvasgraph/canvas_graph.html
Line 1  function canvasGraph(){
          var title = $('#graph_data h1').text();
          var labels = $("#graph_data>ul>li>p[data-name]").map(function(){
            return $(this).attr("data-name");
     5    });
          var percents = $("#graph_data>ul>li>p[data-percent]").map(function(){
            return parseInt($(this).attr("data-percent"));
          });
          var bar = new RGraph.Bar('browsers', percents);
    10    bar.Set('chart.gutter', 50);
          bar.Set('chart.colors', ['red']);
          bar.Set('chart.title', title);
          bar.Set('chart.labels', labels);
          bar.Draw();
    15
        }
```

Browser share for this site

- Safari 4 - 15%

- Internet Explorer - 55%

- Firefox - 14%

- Google Chrome - 16%

Figure 15—Our graph as HTML

First, on line 2, we grab the text for the header. Then, on line 3, we select all the elements that have the data-name attribute. We use jQuery's map function to turn the values from those elements into an array.

We use that same logic again on line 6 to grab an array of the percentages.

With the data collected, RGraph has no trouble drawing our graph.

Displaying Alternative Content

In *Describing Data with HTML*, on page 102, I could have placed the graph between the starting and ending canvas tags. This would hide these elements on browsers that support the canvas while displaying them to browsers that don't. However, the content would still be hidden if the user's browser supports the canvas element but the user has disabled JavaScript.

We simply leave the data outside the canvas and then hide it with jQuery once we've checked that the canvas exists.

```
html5canvasgraph/canvas_graph.html
var canvas = document.getElementById('browsers');
if (canvas.getContext){
  $('#graph_data').hide();
  canvasGraph();
}
```

With that, our graph is ready, except for people using browsers that don't support the canvas element.

Falling Back

When building this solution, we already covered fallbacks for accessibility and lack of JavaScript, but we can create an alternative graph for people who don't have canvas support but can use JavaScript.

jQuery CSS vs. CSS

In this chapter, we used jQuery to apply styles to the elements as we created them. A lot of that style information, such as the colors of labels and the color of the bars, should be offloaded to a separate style sheet, especially if you want to be able to change the styles independently of the script. For a prototype, this approach is fine, but for a production version, always separate presentation, behavior, and content.

There are a ton of graphing libraries out there, but each one has its own way of grabbing data. Bar graphs are just rectangles with specific heights, and we have all the data on the page we need to construct this graph by hand.

html5canvasgraph/canvas_graph.html

```
Line 1  function divGraph(barColor, textColor, width, spacer, lblHeight){
          $('#graph_data ul').hide();
          var container = $("#graph_data");

     5    container.css( {
            "display" : "block",
            "position" : "relative",
            "height": "300px"}
          );

    10
          $("#graph_data>ul>li>p").each(function(i){

            var bar = $("<div>" + $(this).attr("data-percent") + "%</div>");
            var label = $("<div>" + $(this).attr("data-name") + "</div>");
    15
            var commonCSS = {
                        "width": width + "px",
                        "position" : "absolute",
                        "left" : i * (width + spacer) + "px"};
    20
            var barCSS = {
                        "background-color" : barColor,
                        "color" : textColor,
                        "bottom" : lblHeight + "px",
    25                  "height" :  $(this).attr("data-percent") + "%"
            };
            var labelCSS = {"bottom" : "0", "text-align" : "center"};

            bar.css( $.extend(barCSS, commonCSS) );
    30      label.css( $.extend(labelCSS,commonCSS) );

            container.append(bar);
            container.append(label);
          });
    35  }
```

> ϡ/ **Joe asks:**
> ˇᵕˇ **Why Didn't We Try ExplorerCanvas Here?**
>
> ExplorerCanvas, which we talked about in *Falling Back*, on page 99, and RGraph can work really well together. RGraph even bundles a version of ExplorerCanvas in its distribution. However, this combination works only with Internet Explorer 8. If you're working with IE 7 or older, you'll have to use an alternative solution like the one we discussed. I encourage you to keep an eye on ExplorerCanvas, because it is actively maintained. You might even consider hacking on it yourself to make it work for you.

On line 2, we hide the unordered list so that the text values are hidden. We then grab the element containing the graph data and apply some basic CSS styles. We set the positioning of the element to relative on 6, which will let us absolutely position our bar graphs and labels within this container.

Then we loop over the paragraphs in the bulleted list (line 11) and create the bars. Each iteration over the labels creates two div elements, one for the bar itself and another for the label, which we position below it. So, with just a little bit of math and some jQuery, we are able to re-create the graph. Although it doesn't look *exactly* the same, it's close enough to prove the concept.

We then just need to hook it into our canvas detection, like this:

html5canvasgraph/canvas_graph.html
```
var canvas = document.getElementById('browsers');
if (canvas.getContext){
  $('#graph_data').hide();
  canvasGraph();
}
else{
  divGraph("#f00", "#fff", 140, 10, 20);
}
```

You can see the fallback version in Figure 16, *Our graph now displays in Internet Explorer.*, on page 107. With a combination of JavaScript, HTML, and CSS, we've provided a client-side bar graph and statistical information about browser usage to any platform that requires it. Using the canvas has an additional benefit—it got us to start thinking about a fallback solution from the beginning, rather than trying to wedge something in later. That's really good for accessibility.

This is one of the most accessible and versatile methods of graphing data available. You can easily create the visual representation as well as a text-based alternative. This way, everyone can use the important data you're sharing.

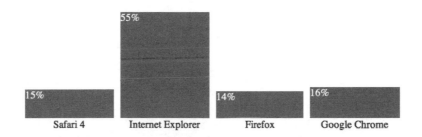

Browser share for this site

Figure 16—Our graph now displays in Internet Explorer.

6.1 The Future

Now that you know a little about how the canvas works, you can start thinking of other ways you might use it. You could use it to create a game, create a user interface for a media player, or use it to build a better image gallery. All you need to start painting is a little bit of JavaScript and a little bit of imagination.

Right now, Flash has an advantage over the canvas because it has wider support, but as HTML5 picks up and the canvas is available to a wider audience, more developers will embrace it for simple 2D graphics in the browser. The canvas doesn't require any additional plug-ins and uses less CPU than Flash, especially on Linux and OS X. Finally, the canvas provides you with a mechanism to do 2D graphics in environments where Flash isn't available. As more platforms support the canvas, you can expect the speed and features to improve, and you'll see more developer tools and libraries appear to help you build amazing things.

But it doesn't stop with 2D graphics. The canvas specification will eventually support 3D graphics as well, and browser manufacturers are implementing hardware acceleration. The canvas will make it possible to create intriguing user interfaces and engaging games using only JavaScript.

CHAPTER 7

Embedding Audio and Video

Audio and video are such an important part of the modern Internet. Podcasts, audio previews, and even how-to videos are everywhere, and until now, they've only been truly usable using browser plug-ins. HTML5 introduces new methods to embed audio and video files into a page. In this chapter, we'll explore a few methods we can use to not only embed the audio and video content but also to ensure that it is available to people using older browsers.

We'll discuss the following two elements in this chapter:[1]

`<audio>` [`<audio src="drums.mp3"></audio>`]
> Play audio natively in the browser. *[C4, F3.6, IE9, S3.2, O10.1, IOS3, A2]*

`<video>` [`<video src="tutorial.m4v"></video>`]
> Play video natively in the browser. *[C4, F3.6, IE9, S3.2, O10.5, IOS3, A2]*

Before we do that, we need to talk about the history of audio and video on the Web. After all, to understand where we're going, we have to understand where we've been.

7.1 A Bit of History

People have been trying to use audio and video on web pages for a long time. It started with people embedding MIDI files on their home pages and using the embed tag to reference the file, like this:

```
<embed src="awesome.mp3" autostart="true"
  loop="true" controller="true"></embed>
```

---

1   In the descriptions that follow, browser support is shown in square brackets using a shorthand code and the minimum supported version number. The codes used are *C:* Google Chrome, *F:* Firefox, *IE:* IE, *O:* Opera, *S:* Safari, *IOS:* iOS devices with Mobile Safari, and *A:* Android Browser.

The embed tag never became a standard, so people started using the object tag instead, which is an accepted W3C standard. To support older browsers that don't understand the object tag, you often see an embed tag nested within the object tag, like this:

```
<object>
<param name="src" value="simpsons.mp3">
<param name="autoplay" value="false">
<param name="controller" value="true">
<embed src="awesome.mp3" autostart="false"
   loop="false" controller="true"></embed>
</object>
```

Not every browser could stream the content this way, though, and not every server was configured properly to serve it correctly. Things got even more complicated when video on the Web became more popular. We went through lots of iterations of audio and video content on the Web, from RealPlayer to Windows Media to QuickTime. Every company had a video strategy, and it seemed like every site used a different method and format for encoding their video on the Web.

Macromedia (now Adobe) realized early on that its Flash Player could be the perfect vehicle for delivering audio and video content across platforms. Flash is available on close to 97 percent of web browsers already. Once content producers discovered they could encode once and play anywhere, thousands of sites turned to Flash streaming for both audio and video.

Then Apple came along in 2007 with the iPhone and iPod touch and decided that Apple would not support Flash on those devices. Content providers responded by making video streams available that would play right in the Mobile Safari browser. These videos, using the H.264 codec, were also playable via the normal Flash Player, which allowed content providers to still encode once while targeting multiple platforms.

The creators of the HTML5 specification believe that the browser should support audio and video natively rather than relying on a plug-in that requires a lot of boilerplate HTML. This is where HTML5 audio and video start to make more sense: by treating audio and video as first-class citizens in terms of web content.

7.2 Containers and Codecs

When we talk about video on the Web, we talk in terms of containers and codecs. You might think of a video you get off your digital camera as an AVI or an MPEG file, but that's actually an oversimplification. Containers are like

Joe asks:

Flash Already Works Across Browsers, So Why Not Use That?

The simple answer is that there are no vendor restrictions on what you as a developer can do with the content once you've embedded it on the page. You can use CSS and JavaScript to manipulate the element, and you don't need to fiddle with parameter passing to the Flash movie. Plus, the situation will improve as the standard becomes more mature.

an envelope that contains audio streams, video streams, and sometimes additional metadata such as subtitles. These audio and video streams need to be encoded, and that's where codecs come in. Video and audio can be encoded in hundreds of different ways, but when it comes to HTML5 video, only a few matter.

Video Codecs

When you watch a video, your video player has to decode it. Unfortunately, the player you're using might not be able to decode the video you want to watch. Some players use software to decode video, which can be slower or more CPU intensive. Other players use hardware decoders and are thus limited to what they can play. Right now, there are three video formats that you need to know about if you want to start using the HTML5 video tag in your work today: H.264, Theora, and VP8.

Codec and Supported Browsers

H.264
    [IE9, S4, C3, IOS]

Theora
    [F3.5, C4, O10]

VP8
    [IE9 (if codec installed), F4, C5, O10.7]

H.264

H.264 is a high-quality codec that was standardized in 2003 and created by the MPEG group. To support low-end devices such as mobile phones, while at the same time handling video for high-definition devices, the H.264 specification is split into various profiles. These profiles share a set of common features, but higher-end profiles offer additional options that improve quality. For example, the iPhone and Flash Player can both play videos encoded with H.264, but the iPhone only supports the lower-quality "baseline" profile, while Flash Player supports higher-quality streams. It's possible to encode a video one time and embed multiple profiles so that it looks nice on various platforms.

H.264 is a de facto standard because of support from Microsoft and Apple, which are licensees. On top of that, Google's YouTube converted its videos to the H.264 codec so it could play on the iPhone, and Adobe's Flash Player supports it as well. However, it's not an open technology. It is patented, and its use is subject to licensing terms. Content producers must pay a royalty to encode videos using H.264, but these royalties do not apply to content that is made freely available to end users.[2]

Proponents of free software are concerned that eventually, the rights holders may begin demanding high royalties from content producers. That concern has led to the creation and promotion of alternative codecs.

Theora

Theora is a royalty-free codec developed by the Xiph.Org Foundation. Although content producers can create videos of similar quality with Theora, device manufacturers have been slow to adopt it. Firefox, Chrome, and Opera can play videos encoded with Theora on any platform without additional software, but Internet Explorer, Safari, and the iOS devices will not. Apple and Microsoft are wary of "submarine patents," a term used to describe patents in which the patent application purposely delays the publication and issuance of the patent in order to lay low while others implement the technology. When the time is right, the patent applicant "emerges" and begins demanding royalties on an unsuspecting market.

VP8

Google's VP8 is a completely open, royalty-free codec with quality similar to H.264. It is supported by Mozilla, Google Chrome, and Opera, and Microsoft's Internet Explorer 9 promises to support VP8 as long as the user has installed a codec already. It's also supported in Adobe's Flash Player, making it an interesting alternative. It is not supported in Safari or the iOS devices, which means that although this codec is free to use, content producers wanting to deliver video content to iPhones or iPads still need to use the H.264 codec.

---

2. http://www.reelseo.com/mpeg-la-announces-avc-h264-free-license-lifetime/

Audio Codecs

As if competing standards for video weren't complicating matters enough, we also have to be concerned with competing standards for audio.

Codec and Supported Browsers

AAC

 [S4, C3, IOS]

MP3

 [IE9, S4, C3, IOS]

Vorbis (OGG)

 [F3, C4, O10]

Advanced Audio Coding (AAC)

This is the audio format that Apple uses in its iTunes Store. It is designed to have better audio quality than MP3s for around the same file size, and it also offers multiple audio profiles similar to H.264. Also, like H.264, it's not a free codec and does have associated licensing fees.

All Apple products play AAC files. So does Adobe's Flash Player and the open source VLC player.

Vorbis (OGG)

This open source royalty-free format is supported by Firefox, Opera, and Chrome. You'll find it used with the Theora and VP8 video codecs as well. Vorbis files have very good audio quality but are not widely supported by hardware music players.

MP3s

The MP3 format, although extremely common and popular, isn't supported in Firefox and Opera because it's also patent-encumbered. It is supported in Safari and Google Chrome.

Video codecs and audio codecs need to be packaged together for distribution and playback. Let's talk about video containers.

Containers and Codecs, Working Together

A container is a metadata file that identifies and interleaves audio or video files. A container doesn't actually contain any information about how the information it contains is encoded. Essentially, a container "wraps" audio and video streams. Containers can often hold any combination of encoded media, but we'll see these combinations when it comes to working with video on the Web:

- The OGG container, with Theora video and Vorbis audio, which will work in Firefox, Chrome, and Opera.

- The MP4 container, with H.264 video and AAC audio, which will work in Safari and Chrome. It will also play through Adobe Flash Player and on iPhones, iPods, and iPads.

- The WebM container, using VP8 video and Vorbis audio, which will work in Firefox, Chrome, Opera, and Adobe Flash Player.

Given that Google and Mozilla are moving ahead with VP8 and WebM, we can eliminate Theora from the mix eventually, but from the looks of things, we're still looking at encoding our videos twice—once for Apple users (who have a small desktop share but a large mobile device share in the United States) and then again for Firefox and Opera users, since both of those browsers refuse to play H.264.[3]

That's a lot to take in, but now that you understand the history and the limitations, let's dig in to some actual implementation, starting with audio.

---

3.   http://lists.whatwg.org/pipermail/whatwg-whatwg.org/2009-June/020620.html

Tip 15

Working with Audio

AwesomeCo is developing a site to showcase some royalty-free audio loops for use in screencasts, and it would like to see a demo page mocked up of a single loop collection. When we're done, we'll have a list of the audio loops, and a visitor will be able to quickly audition each one. We don't have to worry about finding audio loops for this project, because the client's sound engineer has already provided us with the samples we'll need in both MP3 and OGG formats. You can find a small bit of information on how to encode your own audio files in Appendix 3, *Encoding Audio and Video*, on page 231.

Building the Basic List

The audio engineer has provided us with four samples: drums, organ, bass, and guitar. We need to describe each one of these samples using HTML markup. Here's the markup for the drums loop:

html5_audio/audio.html

```
<article class="sample">
  <header><h2>Drums</h2></header>
  <audio id="drums" controls>
    <source src="sounds/ogg/drums.ogg" type="audio/ogg">
    <source src="sounds/mp3/drums.mp3" type="audio/mpeg">
    <a href="sounds/mp3/drums.mp3">Download drums.mp3</a>
  </audio>
</article>
```

We define the audio element first and tell it that we want to have some controls displayed. Next, we define multiple sources for the file. We first define the MP3 and OGG versions of the sample, and then we display a link to allow the visitor to download the MP3 file directly if the browser doesn't support the audio element.

This very basic bit of code will work in Chrome, Safari, and Firefox. Let's put it inside an HTML5 template with the three other sound samples.

html5_audio/audio.html

```
    <article class="sample">
      <header><h2>Drums</h2></header>
      <audio id="drums" controls>
        <source src="sounds/ogg/drums.ogg" type="audio/ogg">
```

```
      <source src="sounds/mp3/drums.mp3" type="audio/mpeg">
      <a href="sounds/mp3/drums.mp3">Download drums.mp3</a>
    </audio>
  </article>

  <article class="sample">
    <header><h2>Guitar</h2></header>
    <audio id="guitar" controls>
      <source src="sounds/ogg/guitar.ogg" type="audio/ogg">
      <source src="sounds/mp3/guitar.mp3" type="audio/mpeg">
      <a href="sounds/mp3/guitar.mp3">Download guitar.mp3</a>
    </audio>
  </article>

  <article class="sample">
    <header><h2>Organ</h2></header>
    <audio id="organ" controls>
      <source src="sounds/ogg/organ.ogg" type="audio/ogg">
      <source src="sounds/mp3/organ.mp3" type="audio/mpeg">
      <a href="sounds/mp3/organ.mp3">Download organ.mp3</a>
    </audio>
  </article>

  <article class="sample">
    <header><h2>Bass</h2></header>
    <audio id="bass" controls>
      <source src="sounds/ogg/bass.ogg" type="audio/ogg">
      <source src="sounds/mp3/bass.mp3" type="audio/mpeg">
      <a href="sounds/mp3/bass.mp3">Download bass.mp3</a>
    </audio>
  </article>
  </body>
</html>
```

When we open the page in an HTML5-compatible browser, each entry in the list will have its own audio player, as you see in Figure 17, *Our page in Safari*, on page 117. The browser itself handles the playback of the audio when you press the Play button.

When we open the page in Internet Explorer, the download links show since the browser doesn't understand the audio element. This makes for a decent fallback solution, but let's see whether we can do better.

Falling Back

Audio fallback support is built into the element itself. We've defined multiple sources for our audio using the source element and have provided links to download the audio files. If the browser cannot render the audio element, it

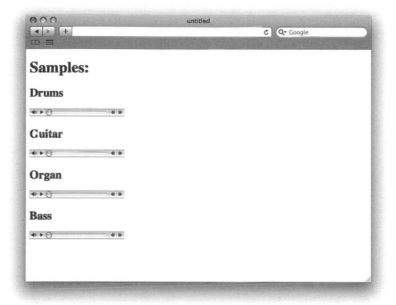

Figure 17—Our page in Safari

will display the link we've placed inside the field. We could even go a step further and use Flash as a fallback after we define our sources.

However, this might not be the best possible approach. You may encounter a browser that supports the audio element but doesn't support the formats you've supplied. For example, you may decide it's not worth your time to provide audio in multiple formats. Additionally, the HTML5 specification specifically mentions that the fallback support for audio is not to be used to place content that would be read by screen readers.

The simplest solution is to move the download link outside the audio element and use JavaScript to hide it, like this:

```
html5_audio/advanced_audio.html
<article class="sample">
  <header><h2>Drums</h2></header>
  <audio id="drums" controls>
    <source src="sounds/ogg/drums.ogg" type="audio/ogg">
    <source src="sounds/mp3/drums.mp3" type="audio/mpeg">
  </audio>
  <a href="sounds/mp3/drums.mp3">Download drums mp3</a>
</article>
```

Then we just need to detect support for audio and hide the links. We do that by creating a new audio element in JavaScript and checking to see whether it responds to the canPlayType() method, like this:

html5_audio/advanced_audio.html
```
var canPlayAudioFiles = !!(document.createElement('audio').canPlayType);
```

We evaluate the response and then hide any anchors that are nested within our sample sections.

html5_audio/advanced_audio.html
```
$(function(){
  var canPlayAudioFiles = !!(document.createElement('audio').canPlayType);

  if(canPlayAudioFiles){
    $(".sample a").hide();
  };
});
```

Fallbacks with audio are relatively easy, and some of your users may actually appreciate the ability to easily download the file.

Playing audio in the browser natively is just the beginning. Browsers are just starting to support the HTML5 JavaScript APIs for audio and video, which you can read about in *Media Content JavaScript API*, on page 123.

Tip 16

Embedding Video

AwesomeCo wants to showcase its new series of training videos on its website, and it wants the videos to be viewable on as many devices as possible, especially on the iPad. As a trial, we've been provided two videos in the "Photoshop Tips" series that we'll use to build a prototype. Thankfully, we've been given the video files in H.264, Theora, and VP8 format, so we can focus on creating the page.[4]

The video tag works exactly like the audio element. We just need to provide our sources, and Chrome, Firefox, Safari, the iPhone, the iPad, and Internet Explorer 9 will display the video without any additional plug-ins. The markup for our first video file, 01_blur, looks like this:

```
html5video/index.html
<article>
  <header>
    <h2>Saturate with Blur</h2>
  </header>
  <video controls>
    <source src="video/h264/01_blur.mp4" />
    <source src="video/theora/01_blur.ogv"/>
    <source src="video/webm/01_blur.webm" />
    <p>Your browser does not support the video tag.</p>
  </video>
</article>
```

We're defining the video tag with controls. We're implicitly telling it that it should not play automatically by *not* including the autoplay attribute.

In order to ensure that web browsers know how to serve our video files, we'll also need to create a new .htaccess file in the same folder as our new web page that defines the MIME types for the videos, like this:

```
html5video/.htaccess
AddType video/ogg  .ogv
AddType video/mp4  .mp4
AddType video/webm .webm
```

---

4. If you want to learn more about encoding your own video files, check out Appendix 3, *Encoding Audio and Video*, on page 231.

Once we upload these files to our web server, our videos will play in a wide variety of browsers, and our users will see a video player similar to the one shown in Figure 18, *Our video displayed using Safari's HTML5 video player*, on page 121.

We still can't reach users of Internet Explorer 8 and older. We'll need to use Flash to make that work.

Falling Back

To properly support a Flash-based fallback and still use HTML5 video, we place the Flash object code within the video tag. The site Video For Everybody[5] outlines this process in detail, but we'll go over a basic implementation here.

Flowplayer[6] is a Flash-based player that can play our already-encoded H.264 video. We'll download the open source version of the player, and we'll place the flowplayer-x.x.x.swf and flowplayer-controls-x.x.x.swf files in our project's swf folder to keep things organized.

We then place this code inside our video tag, right after our last source element:

html5video/index.html

```
<object width="640" height="480" type="application/x-shockwave-flash"
  data="swf/flowplayer-3.2.2.swf">
  <param name="movie" value="swf/flowplayer-3.2.2.swf" />
  <param name="allowfullscreen" value="true" />
  <param name="flashvars"
    value='config={"clip":{"url":"../video/h264/01_blur.mp4",
                          "autoPlay":false,
                          "autoBuffering":true
                          }
                  }' />
  <img src="video/thumbs/01_blur.png"
    width="640" height="264" alt="Poster Image"
    title="No video playback capabilities." />
 </object>
```

Pay close attention to this part:

html5video/index.html

```
<param name="flashvars"
  value='config={"clip":{"url":"../video/h264/01_blur.mp4",
                        "autoPlay":false,
                        "autoBuffering":true
                        }
                }' />
```

---

5.   http://camendesign.com/code/video_for_everybody
6.   http://flowplayer.org/download/index.html

Figure 18—Our video displayed using Safari's HTML5 video player

The video file's source needs to be *relative* to the location of Flowplayer. Since we have placed Flowplayer in the swf folder, we will need to use the path ../video/h264/01_blur.mp4 to get the player to see our video.

We're using *self-closing tags*. As we discussed earlier, we don't usually need to self-close void tags like <img> and <source> in HTML5, but there are a few older web browsers that don't parse the <source> element properly and thus never display the fallback content. Self-closing the <source> elements is the suggested workaround for cases like this.

When we bring up our page in Internet Explorer, our video plays, and we don't need to encode to *another* format, thanks to Flowplayer. Our Internet Explorer friends will see Figure 19, *Our video in Internet Explorer using Flowplayer*, on page 122.[7]

Of course, we still have to come up with a way for people who don't have native video support *and* don't have Flash installed. To make that happen, we'll let people download our video content by adding another section with download links.

html5video/index.html
```
<section class="downloads">
  <header>
    <h3>Downloads</h3>
  </header>
```

---

7. Flash's default security settings may prevent Flowplayer from loading the video unless both the player and the video are served from a web server.

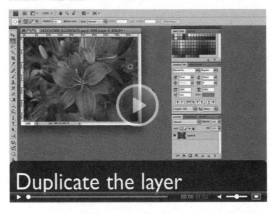

Figure 19—Our video in Internet Explorer using Flowplayer

```
<ul>
  <li><a href="video/h264/01_blur.mp4">H264, playable on most platforms</a></li>
  <li><a href="video/theora/01_blur.ogv">OGG format</a></li>
  <li><a href="video/webm/01_blur.webm">WebM format</a></li>
</ul>
</section>
```

We could use JavaScript to hide these download links if HTML5 video is supported, like this:

```
function canPlayVideo() {
  return !!document.createElement('video').canPlayType;
}
if(canPlayVideo()){
  $(#videos .downloads).hide();
}
```

This uses a detection technique very similar to the one we used in Tip 15, *Working with Audio*, on page 115. In our case, it makes more sense to let people download these videos for use on their iPods or iPads so they can watch them later.

Limitations of HTML5 Video

There are three very important limitations that currently limit the usefulness of HTML5 video.

First, HTML5 video has no provisions for streaming the video files. Users have become accustomed to being able to seek to a specific part of a video. This is something that Flash-based video players excel at, because of the amount of

Media Content JavaScript API

In this chapter, we just briefly touched on the JavaScript APIs for the audio and video elements. The full API can detect the types of audio files the browser can play, and it provides methods to control the playback of the audio elements.

In Tip 15, *Working with Audio*, on page 115, we built a page with multiple sound samples. We could use the JavaScript API to make all the sounds play at (roughly) the same time. Here's a really simplified approach:

```
html5_audio/advanced_audio.html
var element = $("<p><input type='button' value='Play all'/></p>")
element.click(function(){
  $("audio").each(function(){
    this.play();
  })
});

$("body").append(element);
```

We're creating a "Play all" button that, when pressed, cycles through all the audio elements on the page and calls the play() method on each element.

We can do similar things with videos. There are methods to start and pause elements and even query the current time.

Unfortunately, at the time of writing, the JavaScript API isn't well supported everywhere. That shouldn't discourage you from looking at the possibilities outlined in the specification[a] to see what's possible.

a.   http://www.w3.org/TR/html5/video.html#media-elements

effort Adobe has put into Flash as a video delivery platform. To seek with HTML5 video, the file must be downloaded completely on browsers. This may change in time.

Second, there's no way to manage rights. Sites such as Hulu[9] that want to prevent piracy of their content can't rely on HTML5 video. Flash remains a viable solution for these situations.

Finally, and most importantly, the process of encoding videos is costly and time-consuming. The need to encode in multiple formats makes HTML5 video much less attractive. For that reason, you see many sites supplying video in the patent-encumbered H.264 format so that it can be played on the iPod and iPad, using a combination of the HTML5 video tag and Flash.

These issues aren't going to derail HTML5, but they are things to be aware of before we can use HTML5 video to replace Flash as a video delivery vehicle.

9.   http://www.hulu.com

Keep an Eye on the Adult Entertainment Industry

The adult entertainment industry has strongly influenced Internet technology, from e-commerce to the rise of Flash.[a] They're doing so again with HTML5 video.[b] Devices such as the iPhone and iPad are more personal than desktop and laptops, and they don't run Flash. Many adult-oriented websites have already started switching video delivery from Flash to HTML5 with H.264 video for this reason. Interestingly enough, they do not seem to care that HTML5 video currently doesn't provide any rights management.

The adult industry is never afraid to take chances, and you may see some interesting advances in HTML5 video coming as a result of their interest in the technology.

a.   http://chicagopressrelease.com/news/in-tech-world-porn-quietly-leads-the-way
b.   http://news.avn.com/articles/Joone-Points-to-HTML-5-as-Future-of-Web-Content-Delivery-401434.html

Audio, Video, and Accessibility

None of the fallback solutions works really well for users with disabilities. In fact, the HTML5 specification explicitly points that out. A hearing impaired user won't find any value in being able to download the audio file, and a visually impaired user won't have much use for a video file they can view outside of the browser. When we provide content to our users, we should provide usable alternatives whenever possible. Video and audio files should have transcripts that people can view. If you produce your own content, transcripts are easy to make if you plan them from the start because they can come right from the script you write. If a transcript isn't possible, consider a summary that highlights the important parts of the video.

html5video/index.html
```
<section class="transcript">
  <h2>Transcript</h2>
  <p>We'll drag the existing layer to the new button on the bottom of
    the Layers palette to create a new copy.</p>
  <p>Next we'll go to the Filter menu and choose "Gaussian Blur".
    We'll change the blur amount just enough so that we lose a little
    bit of the detail of the image.</p>
  <p>Now we'll double-click on the layer to edit the layer and
    change the blending mode to "Overlay". We can then adjust the
    amount of the effect by changing the opacity slider.</p>
  <p>Now we have a slightly enhanced image.</p>
</section>
```

You can hide the transcript or link to it from the main video page. As long as you make it easy to find and easy to follow, it's going to be really helpful.

7.3   The Future

First-class audio support in the browser opens up a ton of new possibilities for developers. JavaScript web applications can easily trigger sound effects and alerts without having to use Flash to embed the audio. Native video makes it possible to make video available to devices such as iPhones, but it also gives us an open, standard method of interacting with videos using JavaScript. Most importantly, we'll be able to treat video and audio clips just like we treat images, by marking them up semantically and making them easier to identify.

CHAPTER 8

Eye Candy

As web developers, we're always interested in making our user interfaces a little more eye-catching, and CSS3 provides quite a few ways for us to do that. We can use our own custom fonts on our pages. We can create elements with rounded corners and drop shadows. We can use gradients as backgrounds, and we can even rotate elements so things don't look so blocky and boring all the time. We can do all of these things without resorting to Photoshop or other graphics programs, and this chapter will show you how. We'll start off by softening up a form's appearance by rounding some corners. Then, we'll construct a prototype banner for an upcoming trade show, where we'll learn how to add shadows, rotations, gradients, and opacity. Finally, we'll talk about how to use CSS3's @font-face feature so we can use nicer fonts on the company blog.

Specifically, we'll explore the following CSS3 features in this chapter:[1]

border-radius [border-radius: 10px;]
> Rounds corners of elements. *[C4, F3, IE9, S3.2, O10.5]*

RGBa Supprt [background-color: rgba(255,0,0,0.5);]
> Uses RGB color instead of hex codes along with transparency. *[C4, F3.5, IE9, S3.2, O10.1]*

box-shadow [box-shadow: 10px 10px 5px #333;]
> Creates drop shadows on elements. *[C3, F3.5, IE9, S3.2, O10.5]*

Rotation: [transform: rotate(7.5deg);]
> Rotates any element. *[C3, F3.5, IE9, S3.2, O10.5]*

---

1. In the descriptions that follow, browser support is shown in square brackets. The codes used are *C:* Google Chrome, *F:* Firefox, *IE:* Internet Explorer, *O:* Opera, *S:* Safari, *IOS:* iOS devices with Mobile Safari, and *A:* Android Browser.

Gradients: [linear-gradient(top, #fff, #efefef);]
>   Creates gradients for use as images. *[C4, F3.5, S4]*

@font-face [@font-face { font-family: AwesomeFont;]
src: url(http://example.com/awesomeco.ttf); font-weight: bold; }]
>   Allows use of specific fonts via CSS. *[C4, F3.5, IE5+, S3.2, O10.1]*

Tip 17

Rounding Rough Edges

On the Web, everything is a rectangle by default. Form fields, tables, and even sections of web pages all have a blocky, sharp-edged look, so many designers have turned to different techniques over the years to add rounded corners to these elements to soften up the interface a bit.

CSS3 has support for easily rounding corners, and Firefox and Safari have supported this for quite a long time. Unfortunately, Internet Explorer hasn't jumped on board yet. But we can get around that simply enough.

Softening Up a Login Form

The wireframes and mock-ups you received for your current project show form fields with rounded corners. Let's round those corners using only CSS3 first. Our goal is to create something that looks like Figure 20, *Our form with round corners*, on page 130.

For the login form, we'll use some very simple HTML.

css3roughedges/rounded_corners.html

```
<form action="/login" method="post">
  <fieldset id="login">
    <legend>Log in</legend>
    <ol>
      <li>
        <label for="email">Email</label>
        <input id="email" type="email" name="email">
      </li>
      <li>
        <label for="password">Password</label>
        <input id="password" type="password"
               name="password" value="" autocomplete="off"/>
      </li>
      <li><input type="submit" value="Log in"></li>
    </ol>
  </fieldset>
</form>
```

We'll style the form a bit to give it a slightly better look.

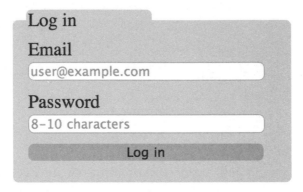

Figure 20—Our form with round corners

css3roughedges/style.css

```css
fieldset{
  width: 216px;
  border: none;
  background-color: #ddd;
}

fieldset legend{
  background-color: #ddd;
  padding: 0 64px 0 2px;
}

fieldset>ol{list-style: none;
  padding:0;
  margin: 2px;
}
fieldset>ol>li{
  margin: 0 0 9px 0;
  padding: 0;
}

/* Make inputs go to their own line */
fieldset input{
  display:block;
}

input{
  width: 200px;
  background-color: #fff;
  border: 1px solid #bbb;
 }
```

```
input[type="submit"]{
  width: 202px;
  padding: 0;
  background-color: #bbb;
}
```

These basic styles remove the bullets from the list and ensure that the input fields are all the same size. With that in place, we can apply the rounding effects to our elements.

Browser-Specific Selectors

Since the CSS3 specification isn't final, browser makers have added some features themselves and have decided to prefix their own implementations. These prefixes let browser makers introduce features early before they become part of a final specification, and since they don't follow the actual specification, the browser makers can implement the actual specification while keeping their own implementation as well. Most of the time, the vendor-prefixed version matches the CSS specification, but occasionally you'll encounter differences. Unfortunately for you, that means you'll need to declare the border radius once for each type of browser.

Firefox uses this selector:

css3roughedges/style.css
```
-moz-border-radius: 5px;
```

WebKit-based browsers, such as Safari and Chrome, use this selector:

css3roughedges/style.css
```
-webkit-border-radius: 5px;
```

To round all the input fields on our form, we need a CSS rule like this:

css3roughedges/style.css
```
input, fieldset, legend{
  border-radius: 5px;
  -moz-border-radius: 5px;
  -webkit-border-radius: 5px;
}
```

Add that to your style.css file, and you have rounded corners.

Falling Back

You have everything working in Firefox, Safari, and Google Chrome, but you know it doesn't work in Internet Explorer and you know it needs to, so you'll need to implement something that gets it as close as possible.

> ## Decide Whether It's Worth the Effort
>
> In our example, the client really wanted rounded corners for all browsers. However, you should always keep these kinds of features optional if you can. Although some people may argue that there's a real benefit to softening up the way the form looks, you should first have an idea of how many people use browsers that don't support CSS-based rounding. If your visitors are mostly Safari and Firefox users, it may not be worth your time to write and maintain a detection and fallback script.

Web developers have been rounding corners for a while now using background images and other techniques, but we're going to keep it as simple as possible. We can detect corner radius with JavaScript and round the corners using any number of rounding techniques. For this example, we'll use jQuery, the jQuery Corner plug-in, and a modification of the Corner plug-in that rounds text fields.

Detecting Rounded Corners Support

Our fallback solution looks very much like the one we used in *Falling Back*, on page 73. We'll include the jQuery library and the plug-in, we'll detect whether the browser supports our attribute, and if it doesn't, we'll activate the plug-in. In this case, we need to detect the presence of the border-radius CSS property, but we also need to check for browser-specific prefixes such as webkit and moz.

Create corner.js, and add this function:

```
css3roughedges/corner.js
function hasBorderRadius(){
  var element = document.documentElement;
  var style = element.style;
  if (style){
    return typeof style.borderRadius == "string" ||
      typeof style.MozBorderRadius == "string" ||
      typeof style.WebkitBorderRadius == "string" ||
      typeof style.KhtmlBorderRadius == "string";
  }
  return null;
}
```

We can now detect whether our browser is missing support for rounded corners, so let's write the code to do the actual rounding. Thankfully, there's a plug-in that can get us started.

jQuery Corners

jQuery Corners[2] is a small plug-in that rounds corners by wrapping elements with additional div tags and styling them so that the target element looks rounded. It doesn't work for form fields; however, with a little imagination, we can use this plug-in and a little bit of jQuery to make it work.

First, grab jQuery Corners, and link to it from your HTML page. While there, also link up your corner.js file.

css3roughedges/rounded_corners.html

```
<script src="jquery.corner.js" charset="utf-8" type='text/javascript'></script>
<script src="corner.js"  charset="utf-8" type='text/javascript'></script>
```

Now we just have to write the code that actually invokes the rounding.

Our formCorners Plug-in

We're going to write a jQuery plug-in so that we can easily apply this rounding to all of the form fields. We already talked about writing jQuery plug-ins in *Falling Back*, on page 43, so I don't need to cover that again. Instead, I'll just walk you through the code for this plug-in, which is based in part on a solution by Tony Amoyal.[3]

Add this to your corners.js file:

css3roughedges/corner.js

```
(function($){
  $.fn.formCorner = function(){
    return this.each(function() {
      var input = $(this);
      var input_background = input.css("background-color");
      var input_border = input.css("border-color");
      input.css("border", "none");
      var wrap_width = parseInt(input.css("width")) + 4;
      var wrapper = input.wrap("<div></div>").parent();
      var border = wrapper.wrap("<div></div>").parent();
      wrapper.css("background-color", input_background)
             .css("padding", "1px");
      border.css("background-color",input_border)
            .css("width", wrap_width + "px")
            .css('padding', '1px');
      wrapper.corner("round 5px");
      border.corner("round 5px");
    });
  };
})(jQuery);
```

---

2.   http://www.malsup.com/jquery/corner/

3.   http://www.tonyamoyal.com/2009/06/23/text-inputs-with-rounded-corners-using-jquery-without-image/

We're taking a jQuery object that could be an element or a collection of elements, and we're wrapping it with two div tags that we then round. We first make the innermost div the same color as the background of the original input, and we turn off the border of the actual form field. Then we wrap that field with another field with its own background color, which is the color of the original input's border color, and give it a little bit of padding. This padding is what makes the border's outline visible. Imagine two pieces of construction paper—a green one that's 4 inches wide and the other a red one that's 3 inches wide. When you place the smaller one atop the larger one, you'll see a green border around the red one. That's how this works.

Invoking the Rounding

With the plug-in and our detection library in place, we can now invoke the rounding.

Add this to the corners.js file:

css3roughedges/corner.js
```
Line 1  $(function(){
     2    if(!hasBorderRadius()){
     3      $("input").formCorner();
     4      $("fieldset").corner("round 5px");
     5      $("legend").corner("round top 5px cc:#fff");
     6    }
     7  });
```

We're rounding the three form fields and the fieldset, and finally, on line 5, we're rounding only the top part of the legend and specifying that the cutout of the corner should use white. The plug-in uses the background color of the parent for its cutaway color, and that's not appropriate here.

If the browser has support for the border-radius property, then it runs our plug-in. If not, then it'll use the CSS we added earlier.

A Minor Nudge

IE treats legends a little differently. We can add in a small style fix for IE that pushes the fieldset's legend up a bit so that it looks the same as it does in Firefox and Chrome.

css3roughedges/rounded_corners.html
```
<link rel="stylesheet" href="style.css" type="text/css" media="screen">
<!--[if IE]>
  <style>
    fieldset legend{margin-top: -10px }
  </style>
<![endif]-->
```

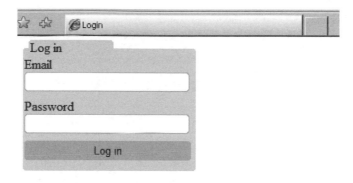

Figure 21—Our forms have round corners in Internet Explorer.

Now things look relatively similar on all of the major browsers; you can see the Internet Explorer version in Figure 21, *Our forms have round corners in Internet Explorer.*, on page 135.

Rounded corners add a bit of softness to your interfaces, and it is extremely easy to use. That said, it's important to be consistent with your use and to not overuse this technique, just like any other aspect of design.

Tip 18

Working with Shadows, Gradients, and Transformations

While rounded corners get a lot of attention, that's just the beginning of what we can do with CSS3. We can add drop shadows to elements to make them stand out from the rest of the content, we can use gradients to make backgrounds look more defined, and we can use transformations to rotate elements. Let's put several of these techniques together to mock up a banner for the upcoming AwesomeConf, a trade show and conference that AwesomeCo puts on each year. The graphic designer has sent over a PSD that looks like Figure 22, *The original concept, which we can re-create using CSS3*, on page 137. We can do the badge, shadow, and even the transparency all in CSS. The only thing we'll need from the graphic designer is the background image of the people.

The Basic Structure

Let's start by marking up the basic structure of the page in HTML.

css3banner/index.html
```html
<div id="conference">

  <section id="badge">
    <h3>Hi, My Name Is</h3>
    <h2>Barney</h2>
  </section>

  <section id="info">
  </section>
</div>
```

We can style the basics with this:

css3banner/style.css
```css
#conference{
  background-color: #000;
  width: 960px;
  float:left;
  background-image: url('images/awesomeconf.jpg');
  background-position: center;
  height: 240px;
}
```

Figure 22—The original concept, which we can re-create using CSS3

```
#badge{
  text-align: center;
  width: 200px;
  border: 2px solid blue;
}

#info{
  margin: 20px;
  padding: 20px;
  width: 660px;
  height: 160px;
}


#badge, #info{
    float: left;
    background-color: #fff;
}


#badge h2{
  margin: 0;
  color: red;
  font-size: 40px;
}

#badge h3{
  margin: 0;
  background-color: blue;
  color: #fff;
}
```

Once we apply that style sheet to our page, we have our badge and content region displayed side by-side, as shown in Figure 23, *Our basic banner*, on page 138, so let's start styling the badge.

Figure 23—Our basic banner

Adding a Gradient

We can add definition to the badge by changing the white background to a subtle gradient that goes from white to light gray. This gradient will work in Firefox, Safari, and Chrome, but the implementation is different for Firefox. Chrome and Safari use WebKit's syntax, which was the original proposal, whereas Firefox uses a syntax that's close to the W3C proposal. Once again, we're using browser prefixes, which you saw in *Browser-Specific Selectors*, on page 131.[4]

```
css3banner/style.css
#badge{
  background-image: -moz-linear-gradient(
    top, #fff, #efefef
  );

  background-image: -webkit-gradient(
    linear,left top, left bottom,
    color-stop(0, #fff),
    color-stop(1, #efefef)
  );

  background-image: linear-gradient(
    top, #fff, #efefef
  );
}
```

Firefox uses the -moz-linear-gradient method, in which we specify the starting point of the gradient, followed by the starting color, and, finally, the ending color.

4.　http://dev.w3.org/csswg/css3-images/#linear-gradients

WebKit-based browsers let us set color stops. In our example, we only need to go from white to gray, but if we needed to add colors, we'd just need to add an additional color stop in the definition.

Adding a Shadow to the Badge

We can easily make the badge appear to be sitting above the banner by adding a drop shadow. Traditionally, we'd do this shadow in Photoshop by adding it to the image or by inserting it as a background image. However, the CSS3 box-shadow property lets us quickly define a shadow on our elements.[5]

We'll apply this rule to our style sheet to give the badge a shadow:

```
css3banner/style.css
#badge{
  -moz-box-shadow: 5px 5px 5px #333;
  -webkit-box-shadow: 5px 5px 5px #333;
  -o-box-shadow: 5px 5px 5px #333;
  box-shadow: 5px 5px 5px #333;
}
```

The box-shadow property has four parameters. The first is the horizontal offset. A positive number means the shadow will fall to the right of the object; a negative number means it falls to the left. The second parameter is the vertical offset. With the vertical offset, positive numbers make the shadow appear below the box, whereas negative values make the shadow appear above the element.

The third parameter is the blur radius. A value of 0 gives a very sharp value, and a higher value makes the shadow blurrier. The final parameter defines the color of the shadow.

You should experiment with these values to get a feel for how they work and to find values that look appropriate to you. When working with shadows, you should take a moment to investigate how shadows work in the physical world. Grab a flashlight and shine it on objects, or go outside and observe how the sun casts shadows on objects. This use of perspective is important, because creating inconsistent shadows can make your interface more confusing, especially if you apply shadows to multiple elements incorrectly. The easiest approach you can take is to use the same settings for each shadow you create.

Rotating the Badge

You can use CSS3 transformations to rotate, scale, and skew elements much like you can with vector graphics programs such as Flash, Illustrator, or

---

5. http://www.w3.org/TR/css3-background/#the-box-shadow

Shadows on Text

In addition to adding styles on elements, you can easily apply shadows to your text as well. It works just like box-shadow.

h1{text-shadow: 2px 2px 2px #bbbbbb;}

You specify the X and Y offsets, the amount of the blur, and the color of the shadow. IE 6, 7, and 8 have support for this as well, using the Shadow filter.

```
filter: Shadow(Color=#bbbbbb,
  Direction=135,
  Strength=3);
```

This is the same approach to apply a drop shadow to an element. Shadows on text create a neat effect, but they can make text harder to read if you make the shadow too strong.

Inkscape.[6] This can help make elements stand out a bit more and is another way to make a web page not look so "boxy." Let's rotate the badge just a bit so it breaks out of the straight edge of the banner.

css3banner/style.css
```
#badge{
  -moz-transform: rotate(-7.5deg);
  -o-transform: rotate(-7.5deg);
  -webkit-transform: rotate(-7.5deg);
  -ms-transform: rotate(-7.5deg);
  transform: rotate(-7.5deg);
}
```

Rotation with CSS3 is pretty simple. All we have to do is provide the degree of rotation, and the rendering just works. All the elements contained within the element we rotate are rotated as well.

Rotating is just as easy as rounding corners, but don't overuse it. The goal of interface design is to make the interface usable. If you rotate elements containing a lot of content, ensure that your viewers can read the content without turning their heads too far in one direction!

Transparent Backgrounds

Graphic designers have used semitransparent layers behind text for quite some time, and that process usually involves either making a complete image in Photoshop or layering a transparent PNG on top of another element with

---

6. http://www.w3.org/TR/css3-2d-transforms/#transform-property

CSS. CSS3 lets us define background colors with a new syntax that supports transparency.

When you first learn about web development, you learn to define your colors using hexadecimal color codes. You define the amount of red, green, and blue using pairs of numbers. 00 is "all off" or "none," and FF is "all on." So, the color red would be FF0000 or "all on for red, all off for blue, and all off for green."

CSS3 introduces the rgb and rgba functions. The rgb function works like the hexadecimal counterpart, but you use values from 0 to 255 for each color. You'd define the color red as rgb(255,0,0).

The rgba function works the same way as the rgb function, but it takes a fourth parameter to define the amount of opacity, from 0 to 1. If you use 0, you'll see no color at all, because it's completely transparent. To make the white box semitransparent, we'll add this style rule:

css3banner/style.css
```
#info{
  background-color: rgba(255,255,255,0.95);
}
```

When working with transparency values like this, your users' contrast settings can sometimes impact the resulting appearance, so experiment with the value and check on multiple displays to ensure you get a consistent result.

While we're working with the info section of our banner, let's round the corners a bit.

css3banner/style.css
```
#info{
  moz-border-radius: 12px;
  webkit-border-radius: 12px;
  o-border-radius: 12px;
  border-radius: 12px;
}
```

With that, our banner looks pretty good in Safari, Firefox, and Chrome. Now let's implement a style sheet for Internet Explorer.

Falling Back

The techniques we used in this section work fine in IE 9, but they're all possible with Internet Explorer 6, 7, and 8 too! We just have to use Microsoft's DirectX filters to pull them off. That means we'll want to rely on a conditional comment to load a specific IE-only style sheet. We'll also need to use JavaScript to create the section element so we can style it with CSS since these versions of IE don't recognize that element natively.

```
css3banner/index.html
    <!--[if lte IE 8]>

    <script>
    document.createElement("section");
    </script>

    <link rel="stylesheet" href="ie.css" type="text/css" media="screen">

    <![endif]-->
  </head>
  <body>
    <div id="conference">

      <section id="badge">
        <h3>Hi, My Name Is</h3>
        <h2>Barney</h2>
      </section>

      <section id="info">
      </section>
    </div>

  </body>
</html>
```

The DirectX filters work in IE 6, 7, and 8, but in IE 8 the filters are invoked differently, so you'll be declaring each of these filters twice. Let's start by looking at how we rotate elements.

Rotation

We can rotate elements using these filters, but it's not as easy as just specifying a degree of rotation. To get the effect we want, we need to use the Matrix filter and specify cosines and sines of the angle we want. Specifically, we need to pass the cosine, the negative value of sine, the sine, and the cosine again,[7] like this:

```
css3banner/filters.css
filter:   progid:DXImageTransform.Microsoft.Matrix(
  sizingMethod='auto expand',
    M11=0.9914448613738104,
    M12=0.13052619222005157,
    M21=-0.13052619222005157,
    M22=0.9914448613738104
  );

-ms-filter: "progid:DXImageTransform.Microsoft.Matrix(
```

---

7. We're doing a linear transformation using a 2x2 matrix.

```
  sizingMethod='auto expand',
    M11=0.9914448613738104,
    M12=0.13052619222005157,
    M21=-0.13052619222005157,
    M22=0.9914448613738104
  )";
```

Complicated? Yes, and more so when you look at the previous example more closely. Remember that our original angle was *negative* 7.5 degrees. So, for our *negative* sine, we need a positive value, and our sine gets a *negative value*.

Math is hard. Let's make gradients instead.

Gradients

IE's Gradient filter works just like the one in the standard, except that you have to type a lot more characters. You provide the starting color and the ending color, and the gradient just shows up.

css3banner/filters.css
```
filter: progid:DXImageTransform.Microsoft.gradient(
    startColorStr=#FFFFFF, endColorStr=#EFEFEF
);
-ms-filter: "progid:DXImageTransform.Microsoft.gradient(
    startColorStr=#FFFFFF, endColorStr=#EFEFEF
)";
```

Unlike the other browsers, you're applying the gradient directly to the element, rather than to the background-image property.

Let's use this filter again to define the transparent background for our info section.

Transparency

The Gradient filter can take extended hexadecimal values for the start and end colors, using the first two digits to define the amount of transparency. We can get very close to the effect we want with this code:

css3banner/filters.css
```
background: none;
filter:
    progid:DXImageTransform.Microsoft.gradient(
    startColorStr=#BBFFFFFF, endColorStr=#BBFFFFFF
);

-ms-filter: "progid:DXImageTransform.Microsoft.gradient(
    startColorStr='#BBFFFFFF', EndColorStr='#BBFFFFFF'
)";
```

These eight-digit hex codes work very much like the rgba function, except that the transparency value comes *first* rather than last. So, we're really looking at alpha, red, green, and blue.

We have to remove the background properties on that element to make this work in IE 7. Now, if you've been following along trying to build this style sheet up, you've noticed that it doesn't actually work yet, but we can fix that.

Putting It All Together

One of the more difficult problems with these IE filters is that we can't define them in pieces. To apply multiple filters to a single element, we have to define the filters as a comma-separated list. Here's what the actual IE style sheet looks like:

```
css3banner/ie.css
#info{
  background: none;
  filter:
    progid:DXImageTransform.Microsoft.gradient(
    startColorStr=#BBFFFFFF, endColorStr=#BBFFFFFF
  );
  -ms-filter: "progid:DXImageTransform.Microsoft.gradient(
    startColorStr='#BBFFFFFF', EndColorStr='#BBFFFFFF'
  )";
}

#badge{
  filter:
    progid:DXImageTransform.Microsoft.Matrix(
    sizingMethod='auto expand',
      M11=0.9914448613738104,
      M12=0.13052619222005157,
      M21=-0.13052619222005157,
      M22=0.9914448613738104
    ),
    progid:DXImageTransform.Microsoft.gradient(
      startColorStr=#FFFFFF, endColorStr=#EFEFEF
    ),
    progid:DXImageTransform.Microsoft.Shadow(
      color=#333333, Direction=135, Strength=3
    );

  -ms-filter: "progid:DXImageTransform.Microsoft.Matrix(
    sizingMethod='auto expand',
      M11=0.9914448613738104,
      M12=0.13052619222005157,
      M21=-0.13052619222005157,
      M22=0.9914448613738104
    ),
```

Figure 24—Our banner as shown in Internet Explorer 8

```
progid:DXImageTransform.Microsoft.gradient(
    startColorStr=#FFFFFF, endColorStr=#EFEFEF
),
progid:DXImageTransform.Microsoft.Shadow(
    color=#333333, Direction=135, Strength=3
)";
}
```

That's a lot of code to get the desired result, but it shows that it is possible to use these features. If you look at Figure 24, *Our banner as shown in Internet Explorer 8*, on page 145, you'll see we got pretty close. All we have to do now is round the corners on the info section, and you can refer to Tip 17, *Rounding Rough Edges*, on page 129 to see how to do that.

Although these filters are clunky and a little bit quirky, you should still investigate them further in your own projects because you'll be able to provide a similar user experience to your IE users.

Remember that the effects we explored in this section are all presentational. When we created the initial style sheet, we made sure to apply background colors so that text would be readable. Browsers that cannot understand the CSS3 syntax can still display the page in a readable manner.

Tip 19

Using Real Fonts

Typography is so important to user experience. The book you're reading right now has fonts that were carefully selected by people who understand how choosing the right fonts and the right spacing can make it much easier for people to read this book. These concepts are just as important to understand on the Web.

The fonts we choose when conveying our message to our readers impact how our readers interpret that message. Here's a font that's perfectly appropriate for a loud heavy-metal band:

But that might not work out so well for the font on the cover of this book:

As you can see, choosing a font that matches your message is really important. The problem with fonts on the Web is that we web developers have been limited to a handful of fonts, commonly known as "web-safe" fonts. These are the fonts that are in wide use across most users' operating systems.

To get around that, we've historically used images for our fonts and either directly added them to our page's markup or used other methods like CSS background images or sIFR,[8] which renders fonts using Flash. CSS3's Fonts module offers a much nicer approach.

@font-face

The @font-face directive was actually introduced as part of the CSS2 specification and was implemented in Internet Explorer 5. However, Microsoft's implementation used a font format called Embedded OpenType (EOT), and most fonts

---

8. http://www.mikeindustries.com/blog/sifr

today are in TrueType or OpenType format. Other browsers support the OpenType and TrueType fonts currently.

AwesomeCo's director of marketing has decided that the company should standardize on a font for both print and the Web. You've been asked to investigate a font called Garogier, a simple, thin font that is completely free for commercial use. As a trial run, we'll apply this font to the blog example we created in Tip 1, *Redefining a Blog Using Semantic Markup*, on page 14. That way, everyone can see the font in action.

Font Formats

Fonts are available in a variety of formats, and the browsers you're targeting will determine what format you'll need to serve to your visitors.

Format and Supported Browsers

Embedded OpenType (EOT)
  [IE5–8]

TrueType (TTF)
  [IE9, F3.5, C4, S4]

OpenType (OTF)
  [IE9, F3.5, C4, S4, O10.5]

Scalable Vector Graphics (SVG)
  [IOS]

Web Open Font (WOFF)
  [IE9, F3.6]

Internet Explorer browsers prior to 9 only support a format called Embedded OpenType (EOT). Other browsers support the more common TrueType and OpenType fonts quite well.

Microsoft, Opera, and Mozilla jointly created the Web Open Font Format, which allows lossless compression and better licensing options for font makers.

To hit all of these browsers, you have to make your fonts available in multiple formats.

Fonts and Rights

Some fonts aren't free. Like stock photography or other copyrighted material, you are expected to comply with the rights and licenses of the material you use on your website. If you purchase a font, you're usually within your rights to use it in your logo and images on your pages. These are called *usage rights*. However, the @font-face approach brings a different kind of licensing into play—redistribution rights.

When you embed a font on your page, your users will have to download that font, meaning your site is now distributing this font to others. You need to be absolutely positive the fonts you're using on your pages allow for this type of usage.

Typekit[a] has a large library of licensed fonts available, and they provide tools and code that make it easy to integrate with your website. They are not a free service, but they are quite affordable if you need to use a specific font.

Google provides the Google Font API[b], which is similar to Typekit but contains only open source fonts.

Both of these services use JavaScript to load the fonts, so you will need to ensure that your content is easy to read for users without JavaScript.

As long as you remember to treat fonts like any other asset, you shouldn't run into any problems.

a. http://www.typekit.com/
b. http://code.google.com/apis/webfonts/

Changing Our Font

The font we're looking at is available at FontSquirrel[11] in TrueType, WOFF, SVG, and EOT formats, which will work just perfectly.

Using the font involves two steps—defining the font and attaching the font to elements. In the style sheet for the blog, add this code:

css3fonts/style.css

```
@font-face {
  font-family: 'GarogierRegular';
  src: url('fonts/Garogier_unhinted-webfont.eot');
  src: url('fonts/Garogier_unhinted-webfont.woff') format('woff'),
       url('fonts/Garogier_unhinted-webfont.ttf') format('truetype'),
       url('fonts/Garogier_unhinted-webfont.svg#webfontew0qE009') format('svg');
  font-weight: normal;
}
```

---

11. You can grab it from http://www.fontsquirrel.com/fonts/Garogier and also in the book's downloadable code.

Joe asks:

How Do I Convert My Own Fonts?

If you have developed your own font or have purchased the rights to a font and need to make it available in multiple formats, the website FontSquirrel has a converter[a] you can use that will provide you with the converted fonts as well as a style sheet with the @font-face code you'll need. Be sure your font's license allows this type of usage, though.

a.   http://www.fontsquirrel.com/fontface/generator

We're defining the font family first, giving it a name, and then supplying the font sources. We're putting the Embedded OpenType version first so that IE sees it right away, and then we provide the other sources. A user's browser is going to just keep trying sources until it finds one that works.

Now that we've defined the font family, we can use it in our style sheet. We'll change our original font style so it looks like this:

```
css3fonts/style.css
body{
  font-family: "GarogierRegular";
}
```

With that simple change, our page's text displays in the new font, like the example in Figure 25, *The blog with the new font applied*, on page 150.

Applying a font is relatively easy in modern browsers, but we need to consider browsers that don't support this yet.

Falling Back

We've already provided fallbacks for various versions of IE and other browsers, but we still need to ensure our pages are readable in browsers that lack support for the @font-face feature.

We provided alternate versions of the Garogier font, but when we applied the font, we didn't specify any fallback fonts. That means if the browser doesn't support displaying our Garogier font, it's just going to use the browser's default font. That might not be ideal.

Font stacks are lists of fonts ordered by priority. You specify the font you *really* want your users to see first and then specify other fonts that are suitable fallbacks afterwards.

AwesomeCo Blog!

<u>Latest Posts</u>   <u>Archives</u>   <u>Contributors</u>   <u>Contact Us</u>

How Many Should We Put You Down For?

Posted by Brian on October 1st, 2010 at 2:39PM

The first big rule in sales is that if the person leaves empty-handed, they're likely not going to come back. That's why you have to be somewhat aggressive when you're working with a customer, but you have to make sure you don't overdo it and scare them away.

"Never give someone a chance to say no when selling your product."

One way you can keep a conversation going is to avoid asking questions that have yes or no answers. For example, if you're selling a service plan, don't ever ask "Are you interested in our 3 or 5 year service plan?"

Figure 25—The blog with the new font applied

When creating a font stack, take the extra time to find truly suitable fallback fonts. Letter spacing, stroke width, and general appearance should be similar. The website UnitInteractive has an excellent article on this.[13]

Let's alter our font like this:

```
css3fonts/style.css
font-family: "GarogierRegular", Georgia,
             "Palatino", "Palatino Linotype",
             "Times", "Times New Roman", serif;
```

We're providing a large array of fallbacks here, which should help us maintain a similar appearance. It's not perfect in all cases, but it's better than relying on the default font, which can sometimes be quite hard to read.

Fonts can go a long way to make your page more attractive and easier to read. Experiment with your own work. There are a large number of fonts, both free and commercial, waiting for you.

8.1 The Future

In this chapter, we explored a few ways CSS3 replaces traditional web development techniques, but we only scratched the surface. The CSS3 specification talks about 3D transformations and even simple animations, meaning that we can use style sheets instead of JavaScript to provide interaction cues to users, much like we do with :hover.

---

13. http://unitinteractive.com/blog/2008/06/26/better-css-font-stacks/

In addition, some browsers are already supporting multiple background images and gradient borders. Finally, keep an eye out for improvements in paged content, such as running headers and footers and page number support.

The CSS3 modules, when completed, will make it much easier for us to create richer, better, and more inviting interface elements for our users, so be sure to keep an eye out for new features.

Part III

Beyond HTML5

CHAPTER 9

Working with Client-Side Data

We have talked about HTML5 and CSS3 markup, but now let's turn our attention to some of the technologies and features associated with HTML5. Cross-document Messaging and offline support, for example, let us communicate across domains and create solutions that let our users work offline.

Some features such as Web Storage, Web SQL Databases, and Web Sockets were spun off from the HTML5 specification. Others, such as Geolocation, were never part of the specification at all, but browser makers and developers have associated Geolocation with HTML5 because the specification is being implemented alongside other features.

This part of the book covers these features, with more attention given to those features that are already usable right now. We'll also spend a chapter discussing things that are coming next. Let's start by looking at Web Storage and Web SQL Storage, two specifications that let us store data on the client.

Remember when cookies were awesome? Neither do I. Cookies have been rather painful to deal with since they came on the scene, but we have put up with the hassle because they've been the only way to store information on the clients' machines.

To use them, we have to name the cookie and set its expiration. This involves a bunch of JavaScript code we wrap in a function so we never have to think about how it actually works, kind of like this:

```
html5_localstorage/setcookie.js
// via http://www.javascripter.net/faq/settinga.htm
function SetCookie(cookieName,cookieValue,nDays) {
 var today = new Date();
 var expire = new Date();
 if (nDays==null || nDays==0) nDays=1;
 expire.setTime(today.getTime() + 3600000*24*nDays);
```

```
document.cookie = cookieName+"="+escape(cookieValue)
                + ";expires="+expire.toGMTString();
}
```

Aside from the hard-to-remember syntax, there are also the security concerns. Some sites use cookies to track users' surfing behavior, so users disable cookies in some fashion.

HTML5 introduced a few new options for storing data on the client: Web Storage (using either localStorage or sessionStorage)[1] and Web SQL Databases.[2] They're easy to use, incredibly powerful, and reasonably secure. Best of all, they're implemented today by several browsers, including iOS's Mobile Safari and Android 2.0's web browser. However, they are no longer part of the HTML5 specification—they've been spun off into their own specifications.

While localStorage, sessionStorage, and Web SQL Databases can't replace cookies intended to be shared between the client and the server—like in the case of web frameworks that use the cookies to maintain state across requests—they can be used to store data that only users care about, such as visual settings or preferences. They also come in handy for building mobile applications that can run in the browser but are not connected to the Internet. Many web applications currently call back to a server to save user data, but with these new storage mechanisms, an Internet connection is no longer an absolute dependency. User data could be stored locally and backed up when necessary.

When you combine these methods with HTML5's new offline features, you can build complete database applications right in the browser that work on a wide variety of platforms, from desktops to iPads and Android phones. In this chapter, you'll learn how to use these techniques to persist user settings and create a simple notes database.

In this chapter, we'll get acquainted with the following features:[3]

localStorage
> Stores data in key/value pairs, tied to a domain, and persists across browser sessions. *[C5, F3.5, S4, IE8, O10.5, IOS, A]*

---

1. http://www.whatwg.org/specs/web-apps/2007-10-26/#storage
2. http://www.whatwg.org/specs/web-apps/2007-10-26/#sql
3. In the descriptions that follow, browser support is shown in square brackets using a shorthand code and the minimum supported version number. The codes used are *C:* Google Chrome, *F:* Firefox, *IE:* Internet Explorer, *O:* Opera, *S:* Safari, *IOS:* iOS devices with Mobile Safari, and *A:* Android Browser.

sessionStorage

> Stores data in key/value pairs, tied to a domain, and is erased when a browser session ends. *[C5, F3.5, S4, IE8, O10.5, IOS, A]*

Web SQL Databases

> Fully relational databases with support for creating tables, inserts, updates, deletes, and selects, with transactions. Tied to a domain and persists across sessions. *[C5, S3.2, O10.5, IOS3.2, A2]*

Offline Web Applications

> Defines files to be cached for offline use, allowing applications to run without an Internet connection. *[C4, S4, F3.5, O10.6, IOS3.2, A2]*

Tip 20

Saving Preferences with localStorage

The localStorage mechanism provides a very simple method for developers to persist data on the client's machine. The localStorage mechanism is simply a name/value store built in to the web browser.

Information stored in localStorage persists between browser sessions and can't be read by other websites, because it's restricted to the domain you're currently visiting.[4]

AwesomeCo is in the process of developing a new customer service portal and wants users to be able to change the text size, background, and text color of the site. Let's implement that using localStorage so that when we save the changes, they persist from one browser session to the next. When we're done, we'll end up with a prototype that looks like Figure 26, *Values for the users' preferences are stored in locally via the localStorage approach.*, on page 159.

Building the Preferences Form

Let's craft a form using some semantic HTML5 markup and some of the new form controls you learned about in Chapter 3, *Creating User-Friendly Web Forms*, on page 31. We want to let the user change the foreground color, change the background color, and adjust their font size.

```
html5_localstorage/index.html
<p><strong>Preferences</strong></p>
<form id="preferences" action="save_prefs"
      method="post" accept-charset="utf-8">
  <fieldset id="colors" class="">
    <legend>Colors</legend>
    <ol>
      <li>
        <label for="background_color">Background color</label>
        <input type="color" name="background_color"
               value="" id="background_color">
      </li>
      <li>
        <label for="text_color">Text color</label>
```

---

4. Just watch out when you're developing things locally. If you're working on localhost, for example, you can easily get your variables mixed up!

Figure 26—Values for the users' preferences are stored in locally via the **localStorage** approach.

```
      <input type="color" name="text_color"
             value="" id="text_color">
  </li>
  <li>
    <label for="text_size">Text size</label>
    <select name="text_size" id="text_size">
      <option value="16">16px</option>
      <option value="20">20px</option>
      <option value="24">24px</option>
      <option value="32">32px</option>
    </select>
  </li>
  </ol>

</fieldset>

<input type="submit" value="Save changes">
</form>
```

We'll just use HTML color codes for the color.

Saving and Loading the Settings

To work with the localStorage system, you use JavaScript to access the window.localStorage() object. Setting a name and value pair is as simple as this:

html5_localstorage/index.html
```
localStorage.setItem("background_color", $("#background_color").val());
```

Grabbing a value back out is just as easy.

html5_localstorage/index.html
```
var bgcolor = localStorage.getItem("background_color");
```

Let's create a method for saving all the settings from the form.

html5_localstorage/index.html
```
function save_settings(){
  localStorage.setItem("background_color", $("#background_color").val());
  localStorage.setItem("text_color", $("#text_color").val());
  localStorage.setItem("text_size", $("#text_size").val());
  apply_preferences_to_page();
}
```

Next, let's build a similar method that will load the data from the localStorage system and place it into the form fields.

html5_localstorage/index.html
```
function load_settings(){
  var bgcolor = localStorage.getItem("background_color");
  var text_color = localStorage.getItem("text_color");
  var text_size = localStorage.getItem("text_size");

  $("#background_color").val(bgcolor);
  $("#text_color").val(text_color);
  $("#text_size").val(text_size);

  apply_preferences_to_page();
}
```

This method also calls a method that will apply the settings to the page itself, which we'll write next.

Applying the Settings

Now that we can retrieve the settings from localStorage, we need to apply them to the page. The preferences we're working with are all related to CSS in some way, and we can use jQuery to modify any element's styles.

html5_localstorage/index.html
```
function apply_preferences_to_page(){
  $("body").css("backgroundColor", $("#background_color").val());
  $("body").css("color", $("#text_color").val());
  $("body").css("fontSize", $("#text_size").val() + "px");
}
```

Finally, we need to fire all of this when the document is ready.

html5_localstorage/index.html
```
$(function(){
  load_settings();

  $('form#preferences').submit(function(event){
    event.preventDefault();
    save_settings();
  });
});
```

> ## sessionStorage
>
> We can use localStorage for things that we want to persist even after our users close their web browsers, but sometimes we need a way to store some information while the browser is open and throw it away once the session is over. That's where session-Storage comes into play. It works the same way as localStorage, but the contents of the sessionStorage are cleared out once the browser session ends. Instead of grabbing the localStorage object, you grab the sessionStorage object
>
> ```
> sessionStorage.setItem('name', 'Brian Hogan');
> var name = sessionStorage.getItem('name');
> ```
>
> Creating a fallback solution for this is as simple as ensuring that the cookies you create expire when the browser closes.

Falling Back

The localStorage method works only on the latest Internet Explorer, Firefox, Chrome, and Safari, so we'll need a fallback method for older browsers. We have a couple of approaches. We can save the information on the server, or we persist the preferences on the client side using cookies.

Server-Side Storage

If you have user accounts in your system, consider making the preferences page persist the settings to the user's record in your application. When they log in, you can check to see whether any client-side settings exist and, if they don't, load them from the server. This way, your users keep their settings across browsers and across computers.

To persist to the server, simply ensure your form posts to the server—don't prevent the default submit behavior with JavaScript if there's no support for cookies.

Server-side storage is really the only method that will work if the user disables JavaScript, because you could code your application to fetch the settings from the database and not the localStorage hash. Also, this is the only approach you can take if you're storing more than 4KB of data, since that's the maximum amount of data you can store in a cookie.

Cookies and JavaScript

The tried-and-true combination of cookies and JavaScript can act as a decent fallback. Using the well-known cookie script from Quirksmode,[5] we can build our own localStorage fallback solution.

---

5.   http://www.quirksmode.org/js/cookies.html

Detecting localStorage support in the browser is pretty simple. We just check for the existence of a localStorage method on the window object:

html5_localstorage/index.html
```
if (!window.localStorage){
}
```

Next, we need methods to write the cookies, which we'll borrow from the Quirksmode article. Add these JavaScript functions to your script block, within the braces:

html5_localstorage/index.html
```
function createCookie(name,value,days) {
  if (days) {
    var date = new Date();
    date.setTime(date.getTime()+(days*24*60*60*1000));
    var expires = "; expires="+date.toGMTString();
  }
  else var expires = "";
  document.cookie = name+"="+value+expires+"; path=/";
}
function readCookie(name) {
  var result = ""
  var nameEQ = name + "=";
  var ca = document.cookie.split(';');
  for(var i=0;i < ca.length;i++) {
    var c = ca[i];
    while (c.charAt(0)==' ') c = c.substring(1,c.length);
    if (c.indexOf(nameEQ) == 0){
      result = c.substring(nameEQ.length,c.length);
    }else{
      result = "";
    }
  }
  return(result);
}
```

Finally, we want to make a localStorage object that uses the cookies as its back end. A very hackish example that barely makes this work might look like this:

html5_localstorage/index.html
```
Line 1 localStorage = (function () {
   2   return {
   3     setItem: function (key, value) {
   4       createCookie(key, value, 3000)
   5     },
   6     getItem: function (key) {
   7       return(readCookie(key));
   8     }
   9   };
  10 })();
```

Take note of line 4. We're creating a cookie with an expiration date of 3,000 days from now. We can't create cookies that never expire, so I'm setting this to a ridiculously long time into the future.

We've kept the basic implementation of localStorage the same from the outside. If you need to remove items or clear everything out, you'll need to get a little more creative. Ideally, in the near future, we can remove this hackish solution and rely only on the browser's localStorage() methods.

Tip 21

Storing Data in a Client-Side Relational Database

The localStorage and sessionStorage methods give us an easy way to store simple name/value pairs on the client's computer, but sometimes we need more than that. The HTML5 specification initially introduced the ability to store data in relational databases. It's since been spun off into a separate specification called Web SQL Storage.[6] If you have even a basic background in writing SQL statements, you'll feel right at home in no time. To get you comfortable, we'll use Web SQL Storage to create, retrieve, update, and destroy notes in a client-side database.

CRUD in Your Browser

The term CRUD, an acronym for "Create, Retrieve, Update, and Delete,"[7] pretty much describes what we can do with our client-side database. The specification and implementations allow us to insert, select, update, and delete records.

AwesomeCo wants to equip their sales team with a simple application to collect notes while they're on the road. This application will need to let users create new notes, as well as update and delete existing ones. To change existing notes, we'll need to let users retrieve them from the database.

Here are the SQL statements we'll need to write in order to make this happen:

Type	Statement
Create a note	INSERT INTO notes (title, note) VALUES("Test", "This is a note");
Retrieve all notes	SELECT id, title, note FROM notes;
Retrieve a specific note	SELECT id, title, note FROM notes where id = 1;
Update a note	UPDATE notes set title = "bar", note = "Changed" where id = 1;
Delete a note	DELETE FROM notes where id = 1;

---

6. http://dev.w3.org/html5/webdatabase/
7. Or "Create, Read, Update, and Destroy," if you prefer

> **Joe asks:**
> ## Isn't the Web SQL Database specification dead?
>
> In November of 2010, the working group that maintains the specification declared that they are not moving forward with the specification and are instead focusing on the IndexedDB specification. We're discussing it in this book because it's already been implemented in Webkit-based browsers, including all iOS and Android devices, Safari, and Google Chrome. Unlike IndexedDB, which isn't implemented anywhere at the time of writing, you can use Web SQL Databases in your projects right now. It may be just the right fit for your needs.

The Notes Interface

The interface for the notes application consists of a left sidebar that will have a list of the notes already taken and a form on the right side with a title field and a larger text area for the note itself. Look at Figure 27, *Our notes application interface*, on page 166 to see what we're building.

To start, we need to code up the interface.

```
html5sql/index.html
<!doctype html>
<html>
  <head>
    <title>AwesomeNotes</title>
    <link rel="stylesheet" href="style.css">
    <script type="text/javascript"
      charset="utf-8"
      src=
      "http://ajax.googleapis.com/ajax/libs/jquery/1.4.2/jquery.min.js">
    </script>
    <script type="text/javascript"
        charset="utf-8" src="javascripts/notes.js">
    </script>
  </head>
  <body>
    <section id="sidebar">
      <input type="button" id="new_button" value="New note">
      <ul id="notes">
      </ul>
    </section>
    <section id="main">
      <form>
        <ol>
          <li>
            <input type="submit" id="save_button" value="Save">
            <input type="submit" id="delete_button" value="Delete">
          </li>
```

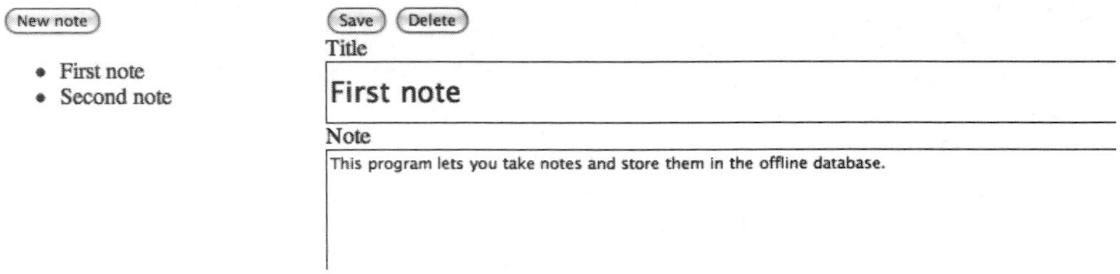

New note

• First note
• Second note

Save   Delete

Title

First note

Note

This program lets you take notes and store them in the offline database.

Figure 27—Our notes application interface

```
      <li>
        <label for="title">Title</label>
        <input type="text" id="title">
      </li>
      <li>
        <label for="note">Note</label>
        <textarea id="note"></textarea>
      </li>
    </ol>
  </form>
  </section>
  </body>
</html>
```

We define the sidebar and main regions using section tags, and we have given IDs to each of the important user interface controls like the Save button. This will make it easier for us to locate elements so that we can attach event listeners.

We'll also need a style sheet so that we can make this look more like the figure. style.css looks like this:

html5sql/style.css
```
#sidebar, #main{
  display: block;
  float: left;
}

#sidebar{
  width: 25%;
}

#main{
  width: 75%;
}
```

```css
form ol{
  list-style: none;
  margin: 0;
  padding: 0;
}

form li{
  padding: 0;
  margin: 0;
}

form li label{
  display:block;
}

#title, #note{
  width: 100%;
  font-size: 20px;
  border: 1px solid #000;
}

#title{
  height: 20px;
}

#note{
  height: 40px;
}
```

This style sheet turns off the bullet points, sizes the text areas, and lays things out in two columns. Now that we have the interface done, we can build the JavaScript we need to make this work.

Connecting to the Database

We need to make a connection and create a database:

```
html5sql/javascripts/notes.js
```
```javascript
// Database reference
var db = null;

// Creates a connection to the local database
connectToDB = function()
{
    db = window.openDatabase('awesome_notes', '1.0',
                             'AwesomeNotes Database', 1024*1024*3);
};
```

We're declaring the db variable at the top of our script. Doing this makes it available to the rest of the methods we'll create.[8] We then declare the method to connect to the database by using the window.openDatabase method. This method takes the name of the database, a version number, a description, and a size parameter.

Creating the Notes Table

Our notes table needs three columns:

Field	Description
id	Uniquely identifies the note. Primary key, integer, auto-incrementing.
title	The title of the note, for easy reference.
Note	The note itself.

Let's create a method to create this table:

```
html5sql/javascripts/notes.js
createNotesTable = function()
{
  db.transaction(function(tx){
    tx.executeSql(
      "CREATE TABLE notes (id INTEGER \
       PRIMARY KEY, title TEXT, note TEXT)", [],
      function(){ alert('Notes database created successfully!'); },
      function(tx, error){ alert(error.message); } );
  });
};
```

We fire the SQL statement inside a transaction, and the transaction has two callback methods: one for a successful execution and one for a failure. This is the pattern we'll use for each of our actions.

Note that the executeSql() method also takes an array as its second parameter. This array is for binding placeholders in the SQL to variables. This lets us avoid string concatenation and is similar to prepared statements in other languages. In this case, the array is empty because we have no placeholders in our query to populate.

Now that we have our first table, we can make this application actually do something.

---

8.   This puts the variable into the global scope, and that's not always a good idea. For this example, we're keeping the JavaScript code as simple as possible.

Loading Notes

When the application loads, we want to connect to the database, create the table if it doesn't already exist, and then fetch any existing notes from the database.

```
html5sql/javascripts/notes.js
// loads all records from the notes table of the database;
fetchNotes = function(){
  db.transaction(function(tx) {
      tx.executeSql('SELECT id, title, note FROM notes', [],
        function(SQLTransaction, data){
          for (var i = 0; i < data.rows.length; ++i) {
              var row = data.rows.item(i);
              var id = row['id'];
              var title = row['title'];

              addToNotesList(id, title);
          }
      });
  });
};
```

This method grabs the results from the database. If it's successful, it loops over the results and calls the addNoteToList method that we define to look like this:

```
html5sql/javascripts/notes.js
// Adds the list item to the list of notes, given an id and a title.
addToNotesList = function(id, title){
  var notes = $("#notes");
  var item = $("<li>");
  item.attr("data-id", id);
  item.html(title);
  notes.append(item);
};
```

We're embedding the ID of the record into a custom data attribute. We'll use that ID to locate the record to load when the user clicks the list item. We then add the new list item we create to the unordered list in our interface with the ID of notes. Now we need to add code to load that item into the form when we select a note from this list.

Fetching a Specific Record

We could add a click event to each list item, but a more practical approach is to watch any clicks on the unordered list and then determine which one was clicked. This way, when we add new entries to the list (like when we add a new note), we don't have to add the click event to the list.

Within our jQuery function, we'll add this code:

```
html5sql/javascripts/notes.js
$("#notes").click(function(event){
  if ($(event.target).is('li')) {
    var element = $(event.target);
    loadNote(element.attr("data-id"));
  }
});
```

This fires off the loadNote() method, which looks like this:

```
html5sql/javascripts/notes.js
loadNote = function(id){
  db.transaction(function(tx) {
    tx.executeSql('SELECT id, title, note FROM notes where id = ?', [id],
      function(SQLTransaction, data){
        var row = data.rows.item(0);
        var title = $("#title");
        var note = $("#note");
        title.val(row["title"]);
        title.attr("data-id", row["id"]);
        note.val(row["note"]);
        $("#delete_button").show();
      });
  });
}
```

This method looks a lot like the previous fetchNotes() method. It fires a SQL statement, and we then handle the success path. This time, the statement contains a question-mark placeholder, and the actual value is in the second parameter as a member of the array.

When we have found a record, we display it in the form. This method also activates the Delete button and embeds the ID of the record into a custom data attribute so that updates can easily be handled. Our Save button will check for the existence of the ID. If one exists, we'll update the record. If one is missing, we'll assume it's a new record. Let's write that bit of logic next.

Inserting, Updating, and Deleting Records

When a user clicks the Save button, we want to trigger code to either insert a new record or update the existing one. We'll add a click event handler to the Save button by placing this code inside the jQuery function:

```
html5sql/javascripts/notes.js
$("#save_button").click(function(event){
  event.preventDefault();
  var title = $("#title");
  var note = $("#note");
```

```
  if(title.attr("data-id")){
    updateNote(title, note);
  }else{
    insertNote(title, note);
  }
});
```

This method checks the data-id attribute of the form's title field. If it has no ID, the form assumes we're inserting a new record and invokes the insertNote method, which looks like this:

html5sql/javascripts/notes.js

```
insertNote = function(title, note)
{
  db.transaction(function(tx){
    tx.executeSql("INSERT INTO notes (title, note) VALUES (?, ?)",
                  [title.val(), note.val()],
      function(tx, result){
       var id = result.insertId ;
       alert('Record ' + id+ ' saved!');
       title.attr("data-id", result.insertId );
       addToNotesList(id, title.val());
       $("#delete_button").show();
      },
      function(){
       alert('The note could not be saved.');
      }
    );
  });
};
```

The insertNote() method inserts the record into the database and uses the insertId property of the resultset to get the ID that was just inserted. We then apply this to the "title" form field as a custom data attribute and invoke the addToNotesList() method to add the note to our list on the side of the page.

Next, we need to handle updates. The updateNote() method looks just like the rest of the methods we've added so far:

html5sql/javascripts/notes.js

```
updateNote = function(title, note)
{
  var id = title.attr("data-id");
  db.transaction(function(tx){
   tx.executeSql("UPDATE notes set title = ?, note = ? where id = ?",
                 [title.val(), note.val(), id],
     function(tx, result){
       alert('Record ' + id + ' updated!');
       $("#notes>li[data-id=" + id + "]").html(title.val());
     },
```

```
    function(){
      alert('The note was not updated!');
    }
  );
});
};
```

When the update statement is successful, we update the title of the note in our list of notes by finding the element with the data-id field with the value of the ID we just updated.

As for deleting records, it's almost the same. We need a handler for the delete event like this:

html5sql/javascripts/notes.js
```
$("#delete_button").click(function(event){
  event.preventDefault();
  var title = $("#title");
  deleteNote(title);
});
```

Then we need the delete method itself, which not only removes the record from the database but also removes it from the list of notes in the sidebar.

html5sql/javascripts/notes.js
```
deleteNote = function(title)
{
  var id = title.attr("data-id");
  db.transaction(function(tx){
    tx.executeSql("DELETE from notes where id = ?", [id],
      function(tx, result){
        alert('Record ' + id + ' deleted!');
        $("#notes>li[data-id=" + id + "]").remove();
      },
      function(){
        alert('The note was not deleted!');
      }
    );
  });
};
```

Now we just need to clear out the form so we can create a new record without accidentally duplicating an existing one.

Wrapping Up

Our notes application is mostly complete. We just have to activate the New button, which clears the form out when clicked so a user can create a new note after they've edited an existing one. We'll use the same pattern as we did before—we'll start with the event handler inside the jQuery function for the New button:

```
html5sql/javascripts/notes.js
$("#new_button").click(function(event){
  event.preventDefault();
  newNote();
});
```

Next we'll clear out the data-id attribute of the "title" field and remove the values from the forms. We'll also hide the Delete button from the interface.

```
html5sql/javascripts/notes.js
newNote = function(){
  $("#delete_button").hide();
  var title = $("#title");
  title.removeAttr("data-id");
  title.val("");
  var note = $("#note");
  note.val("");
}
```

We should call this newForm method from within our jQuery function when the page loads so that the form is ready to be used. This way, the Delete button is hidden too.

That's all there is to it. Our application works on iPhones, Android devices, and desktop machines running Chrome, Safari, and Opera. However, there's little chance this will ever work in Firefox, and it's not supported in Internet Explorer either.

Falling Back

Unlike our other solutions, there are no good libraries available that would let us implement SQL storage ourselves, so we have no way to provide support to Internet Explorer users natively. However, if this type of application is something you think could be useful, you could convince your users to use Google Chrome, which works on all platforms, for this specific application. That's not an unheard of practice, especially if using an alternative browser allows you to build an internal application that could be made to work on mobile devices as well.

Another alternative is to use the Google Chrome Frame plug-in.[9] Add this to the top of your HTML page right below the head tag:

---

9.   http://code.google.com/chrome/chromeframe/

html5sql/index.html

```html
<meta http-equiv="X-UA-Compatible" content="chrome=1">
```

This snippet gets read by the Google Chrome Frame plug-in and activates it for this page.

If you want to detect the presence of the plug-in and prompt your users to install it if it doesn't exist, you can add this snippet right above the closing body tag:

html5sql/index.html

```html
<script type="text/javascript"
 src=
 "http://ajax.googleapis.com/ajax/libs/chrome-frame/1/CFInstall.min.js">
</script>

<script>
 window.attachEvent("onload", function() {
   CFInstall.check({
     mode: "inline", // the default
     node: "prompt"
   });
 });
</script>
```

This will give the user an option to install the plug-in so they can work with your site.

Google Chrome Frame may not be a viable solution for a web application meant to be used by the general public, but it works well for internal applications like the one we just wrote. There may be corporate IT policies that prohibit something like this, but I'll leave that up to you to work out how you can get something like this approved if you're in that situation. Installing a plug-in is certainly more cost-effective than writing your own SQL database system.

Tip 22

Working Offline

With HTML5's Offline support,[10] we can use HTML and related technologies to build applications that can still function while disconnected from the Internet. This is especially useful for developing applications for mobile devices that may drop connections.

This technique works in Firefox, Chrome, and Safari, as well as on the iOS and Android 2.0 devices, but there's no fallback solution that will work to provide offline support for Internet Explorer.

AwesomeCo just bought its sales team some iPads, and they'd like to make the notes application we developed in Tip 21, *Storing Data in a Client-Side Relational Database*, on page 164, work offline. Thanks to the HTML5 manifest file, that will be a simple task.

Defining a Cache with the Manifest

The manifest file contains a list of all the web application's client-side files that need to exist in the client browser's cache in order to work offline. *Every* file that the application will reference needs to be listed here in order for things to work properly. The only exception to this is that the file that includes the manifest doesn't need to be listed; it is cached implicitly.

Create a file called notes.manifest. Its contents should look like this:

html5offline/notes.manifest
```
CACHE MANIFEST
# v = 1.0.0
/style.css
/javascripts/notes.js
/javascripts/jquery.min.js
```

The version comment in this file gives us something we can change so that browsers will know that they should fetch new versions of our files. When we change our code, we need to modify the manifest.

---

10. http://www.w3.org/TR/html5/offline.html

Also, we've been letting Google host jQuery for us, but that won't work if we want our application to work offline, so we need to download jQuery and modify our script tag to load jQuery from our javascripts folder.

html5offline/index.html
```
<script type="text/javascript"
  charset="utf-8"
  src="javascripts/jquery.min.js">
</script>
```

Next, we need to link the manifest file to our HTML document. We do this by changing the html element to this:

html5offline/index.html
```
<html manifest="notes.manifest">
```

That's all we need to do. There's just one little catch—the manifest file has to be served by a web server, because the manifest must be served using the text/cache-manifest MIME type. If you're using Apache, you can set the MIME type in an .htaccess like this:

html5offline/.htaccess
```
AddType text/cache-manifest .manifest
```

After we request our notes application the first time, the files listed in the manifest get downloaded and cached. We can then disconnect from the network and use this application offline as many times as we want.

Be sure to investigate the specification. The manifest file has more complex options you can use. For example, you can specify that certain things should not be cached and should never be accessed offline, which is useful for ignoring certain dynamic files.

Manifest and Caching

When you're working with your application in development mode, you are going to want to disable any caching on your web server. By default, many web servers cache files by setting headers that tell browsers not to fetch a new copy of a file for a given time. This can trip you up while you're adding things to your manifest file.

If you use Apache, you can disable caching by adding this to your .htaccess file.

html5offline/.htaccess
```
ExpiresActive On
ExpiresDefault "access"
```

This disables caching on the entire directory, so it's not something you want to do in production. But this will ensure that your browser will always request a new version of your manifest file.

If you change a file listed in your manifest, you'll want to modify the manifest file too, by changing the version number comment we added.

9.1 The Future

Features like localStorage and Web SQL Databases give developers the ability to build applications in the browser that don't have to be connected to a web server. Applications like the ones we worked on run on an iPad or Android device as well, and when we combine them with the HTML5 manifest file, we can build offline rich applications using familiar tools instead of proprietary platforms. As more browsers enable support, developers will be able to leverage them more, creating applications that run on multiple platforms and devices, that store data locally, and that could sync up when connected.

The future of Web SQL Storage is unknown. Mozilla has no plans to implement it in Firefox, and the W3C is choosing instead to move forward implementing the IndexedDB specification. We'll talk more about that specification in Section 11.5, *Indexed Database API*, on page 211. However, Web SQL Storage has been in use on the iOS and Android devices for a while, and it's likely to stay. This specification could be extremely useful to you if you're developing applications in that space.

CHAPTER 10

Playing Nicely with Other APIs

Many interesting APIs that started out as part of the HTML5 specification were eventually spun off into their own projects. Others have become so associated with HTML5 that sometimes it's hard for developers (and even authors) to really tell the difference. In this chapter, we'll talk about those APIs. We'll spend a little time working with the HTML5 history API, and then we'll make pages on different servers talk with Cross-document Messaging, Then we'll look at Web Sockets and Geolocation, two very powerful APIs that can help you make even more interactive applications.

We'll use the following APIs to build those applications:[1]

History
>   Manages the browser history. *[C5, S4, IE8, F3, O10.1 IOS3.2, A2]*

Cross-document Messaging
>   Sends messages between windows with content loaded on different domains. *[C5, S5, F4, IOS4.1, A2]*

Web Sockets
>   Creates a stateful connection between a browser and a server. *[C5, S5, F4, IOS4.2]*

Geolocation
>   Gets latitude and longitude from the client's browser. *[C5, S5, F3.5, O10.6, IOS3.2, A2]*

---

1. In the descriptions that follow, browser support is shown in square brackets using a shorthand code and the minimum supported version number. The codes used are *C*: Google Chrome, *F*: Firefox, *IE*: Internet Explorer, *O*: Opera, *S*: Safari, *IOS*: iOS devices with Mobile Safari, and *A*: Android Browser.

Tip 23

Preserving History

The HTML5 specification introduces an API to manage the browser history.[2] In Tip 12, *Creating an Accessible Updatable Region*, on page 86, we built a prototype for AwesomeCo's new home page that switched out the main content when we clicked one of the navigation tabs. One drawback with the approach we used is that there's no support for the browser's Back button. We can fix that with some hacks, but we will eventually be able to solve it for good with the History API.

We can detect support for this API like this:

html5history/javascripts/application.js
```
function supportsHistory(){
  return !!(window.history && window.history.pushState);
}
```

We use this method whenever we need to work with the History objects.

Storing the Current State

When a visitor brings up a new web page, the browser adds that page to its history. When a user brings up a new tab, we need to add the new tab to the history ourselves, like this:

html5history/javascripts/application.js
```
Line 1  $("nav ul").click(function(event){
          target = $(event.target);
          if(target.is("a")){
            event.preventDefault();
     5      if ( $(target.attr("href")).hasClass("hidden") ){

              if(supportsHistory()){
                var tab = $(target).attr("href");
                var stateObject = {tab: tab};
    10          window.history.pushState(stateObject, tab);
              };

              $(".visible").removeClass("visible").addClass("hidden").hide();
              $(target.attr("href")).removeClass("hidden").addClass("visible").show();
```

---

2. http://www.w3.org/TR/html5/history.html

```
15      };
      };
    });
  });
```

We snag the ID of the element that's visible, and then we add a history state to the browser. The first parameter of the pushstate() method is an object that we'll be able to interact with later. We'll use this to store the ID of the tab we want to display when our user navigates back to this point. For example, when the user clicks the Services tab, we'll store #services in the state object.

The second parameter is a title that we can use to identify the state in our history. It has nothing to do with the title element of the page; it's just a way to identify the entry in the browser's history. We'll use the ID of the tab again.

Retrieving the Previous State

Although this adds a history state, we still have to write the code to handle the history state change. When the user clicks the Back button, the window.onpopstate() event gets fired. We use this hook to display the tab we stored in the state object.

```
html5history/javascripts/application.js
if(supportsHistory()){
  window.onpopstate = function(event) {
    if(event.state){
      var tab = (event.state["tab"]);
      $(".visible")
        .removeClass("visible")
        .addClass("hidden")
        .hide();
      $(tab)
        .removeClass("hidden")
        .addClass("visible")
        .show();
    }
  };
};
```

We fetch the name of the tab and then use jQuery to locate the element to hide by its ID. The code that hides and shows the tabs is repeated here from the original code. We should refactor this to remove the duplication.

Defaulting

When we first bring up our page, our history state is going to be null, so we'll need to set it ourselves. We can do that right above where we defined our window.onpopstate() method.

```
html5history/javascripts/application.js
if(supportsHistory()){
➤   window.history.pushState( {tab: "#welcome"}, '#welcome');
    window.onpopstate = function(event) {
      if(event.state){
        var tab = (event.state["tab"]);
        $(".visible")
          .removeClass("visible")
          .addClass("hidden")
          .hide();
        $(tab)
          .removeClass("hidden")
          .addClass("visible")
          .show();
      }
    };
};
```

Now, when we bring up the page, we can cycle through our tabs using the browser history.[3]

Falling Back

This works in Firefox 4 and Safari 4, as well as in Chrome 5, but it doesn't work in Internet Explorer. Solutions like the jQuery Address plug-in[4] provide the same functionality, but we won't go into implementing that as a fallback solution because it's less of a fallback and more of a complete replacement with a lot of additional features. Keep an eye on browser support for history manipulation, though, because you'll be able to easily provide much more user-friendly applications when you can use this API in every browser.

---

3. You'll want to constantly close your browser and clear your history when testing this. It can be quite painful at times.

4. http://www.asual.com/jquery/address

Tip 24

Talking Across Domains

Client-side web applications have always been restricted from talking directly to scripts on other domains, a restriction designed to protect users.[5] There are numerous clever ways around this restriction, including the use of server-side proxies and clever URL hacks. But now there's a better way.

The HTML5 specification introduced *Cross-document Messaging*, an API that makes it possible for scripts hosted on different domains to pass messages back and forth. For example, we can have a form on http://support.awesomecompany.com post content to another window or iframe whose content is hosted on http://www.awesomecompany.com. It turns out that for our current project, we need to do just that.

AwesomeCo's new support site will have a contact form, and the support manager wants to list all the support contacts and their email addresses next to the contact form. The support contacts will eventually come from a content management system on another server, so we can embed the contact list alongside the form using an iframe. The catch is that the support manager would love it if we could let users click a name from the contact list and have the email automatically added to our form.

We can do this quite easily, but you'll need to use web servers to properly test everything on your own setup. The examples we're working on here don't work in every browser unless we use a server. See *Simple Web Servers*, on page 184 for more on this.

The Contact List

We'll create the contact list first. Our basic markup will look like this:

```
html5xdomain/contactlist/public/index.html
<ul id="contacts">
  <li>
    <h2>Sales</h2>
    <p class="name">James Norris</p>
    <p class="email">j.norris@awesomeco.com</p>
```

---

5. This is known as the Same Origin Policy and is explained more at https://developer.mozilla.org/en/Same_origin_policy_for_JavaScript.

Simple Web Servers

If you don't want to go through the trouble of configuring Apache instances or setting up your own servers, you can use the simple Ruby-based servers included in the book's example code files. For instructions on getting Ruby working on your system, see the file RUBY_README.txt within the book's source code files.

To start the servers, first go into the html5xdomain/contactlist and run the server.rb file like this:

```
ruby server.rb
```

It will start on port 4567. You can then do the same for the server.rb in html5xdomain/supportpage, which will start on port 3000. You can edit the port for each of these by editing the server.rb file.

```
    </li>
    <li>
      <h2>Operations</h2>
      <p class="name">Tony Raymond</p>
      <p class="email">t.raymond@awesomeco.com</p>
    </li>
    <li>
      <h2>Accounts Payable</h2>
      <p class="name">Clark Greenwood</p>
      <p class="email">c.greenwood@awesomeco.com</p>
    </li>
    <li>
      <h2>Accounts Receivable</h2>
      <p class="name">Herbert Whitmore</p>
      <p class="email">h.whitmore@awesomeco.com</p>
    </li>
</ul>
```

On that page, we'll also load both the jQuery library and our own custom application.js file and a simple style sheet. We'll place this in our head section:

html5xdomain/contactlist/public/index.html
```
<script type="text/javascript"
  charset="utf-8"
  src="http://ajax.googleapis.com/ajax/libs/jquery/1.4.2/jquery.min.js">
</script>

<script type="text/javascript"
  src="javascripts/application.js">
</script>
<link rel="stylesheet" href="style.css" type="text/css" media="screen">
```

The style sheet for the contact list looks like this:

```
html5xdomain/contactlist/public/style.css
ul{
  list-style: none;
}

ul h2, ul p{margin: 0;}
ul li{margin-bottom: 20px;}
```

It's just a couple of small tweaks to make the list look a little cleaner.

Posting the Message

When a user clicks an entry in our contact list, we'll grab the email from the list item and post a message back to the parent window. The postMessage() method takes two parameters: the message itself and the target window's origin. Here's how the entire event handler looks:

```
html5xdomain/contactlist/public/javascripts/application.js
$(function(){
  $("#contacts li").click(function(event){
    var email = ($(this).find(".email").html());
    var origin = "http://192.168.1.244:3000/index.html";
      window.parent.postMessage(email, origin);
  });
});
```

You'll need to change the origin if you're following along, since it has to match the URL of the parent window.[6]

Now we need to implement the page that will hold this frame and receive its messages.

The Support Site

The support site's structure is going to look very similar, but to keep things separate, we should work in a different folder, especially since this site will need to be placed on a different web server. We'll need to make sure you include links to a style sheet, jQuery, and a new application.js file.

Our support page needs a contact form and an iframe that points to our contact list. We'll do something like this:

```
html5xdomain/supportpage/public/index.html
<div id="form">
  <form id="supportform">
    <fieldset>
      <ol>
```

---

6. That's not entirely true. You can use just the domain or even a wildcard. But our fall-back solution requires the complete URL, and it's also good security.

```
        <li>
          <label for="to">To</label>
          <input type="email" name="to" id="to">
        </li>
        <li>
          <label for="from">From</label>
          <input type="text" name="from" id="from">
        </li>
        <li>
          <label for="message">Message</label>
          <textarea name="message" id="message"></textarea>
        </li>
      </ol>
      <input type="submit" value="Send!">
    </fieldset>
  </form>
 </div>

<div id="contacts">
  <iframe src="http://192.168.1.244:4567/index.html"></iframe>
</div>
```

We'll style it up with this CSS that we add to style.css:

html5xdomain/supportpage/public/style.css
```
#form{
  width: 400px;
  float: left;
}

#contacts{
  width: 200px;
  float: left;
}

#contacts iframe{
  border: none;
  height: 400px;
}

fieldset{
  width: 400px;
  border: none;
}

fieldset legend{
  background-color: #ddd;
  padding: 0 64px 0 2px;
}
```

```
fieldset>ol{
  list-style: none;
  padding: 0;
  margin: 2px;
}

fieldset>ol>li{
  margin: 0 0 9px 0;
  padding: 0;
}

/* Make inputs go to their own line */
fieldset input, fieldset textarea{
  display:block;
  width: 380px;
}
fieldset input[type=submit]{
  width: 390px;
}

fieldset textarea{
  height: 100px;
}
```

This places the form and the iframe side by side and modifies the form so it looks like Figure 28, *Our completed support site*, on page 188.

Receiving the Messages

The onmessage event fires whenever the current window receives a message. The message comes back as a property of the event. We'll register this event using jQuery's bind() method so it works the same in all browsers.

html5xdomain/supportpage/public/javascripts/application.js
```
$(function(){
    $(window).bind("message",function(event){
      $("#to").val(event.originalEvent.data);
    });

});
```

jQuery's bind() method wraps the event and doesn't expose every property. We can get what we need by accessing it through the event's originalEvent property instead.

If you open this in Firefox, Chrome, Safari, or Internet Explorer 8, you'll see that it works extremely well. Now let's make it work for IE 6 and 7.

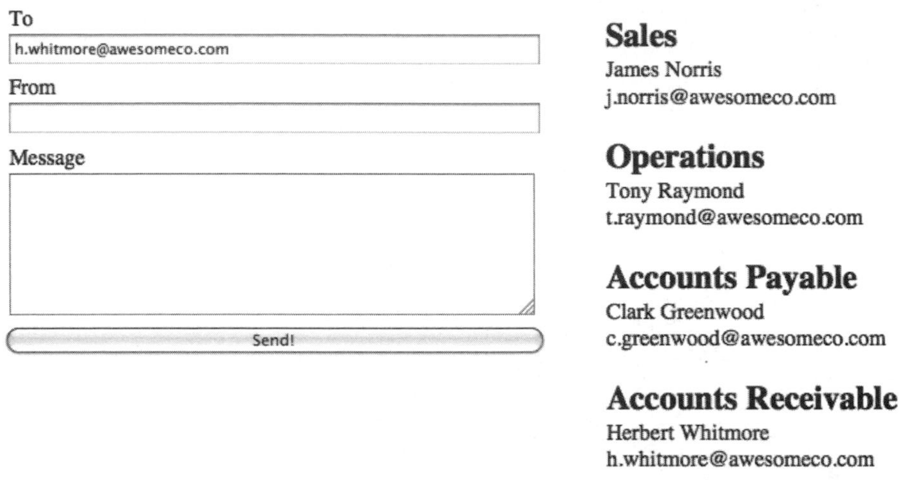

To

h.whitmore@awesomeco.com

From

Message

Send!

Sales

James Norris
j.norris@awesomeco.com

Operations

Tony Raymond
t.raymond@awesomeco.com

Accounts Payable

Clark Greenwood
c.greenwood@awesomeco.com

Accounts Receivable

Herbert Whitmore
h.whitmore@awesomeco.com

Figure 28—Our completed support site

Falling Back

To support IE 6 and 7, we'll use the jQuery Postback plug-in, which emulates cross-domain messaging. We'll use jQuery's getScript() method to pull that library in only when we need it. To do that, we'll just detect whether the postMessage() method exists.

First, we'll modify our contact list.

```
html5xdomain/contactlist/public/javascripts/application.js
//START_HIGHLIGHTING
if(window.postMessage){
//END_HIGHLIGHTING
  window.parent.postMessage(email, origin);
  //START_HIGHLIGHTING
}else{
  $.getScript("javascripts/jquery.postmessage.js", function(){
    $.postMessage(email, origin, window.parent);
  });
}
//END_HIGHLIGHTING
```

The jQuery Postmessage plug-in adds a postMessage() method, which works almost exactly like the standard postMessage() method.

Now, let's turn our attention to the support site. We'll use the same approach here, pulling in the library and calling the newly added re-ceiveMessage() method.

html5xdomain/supportpage/public/javascripts/application.js

```
➤ if(window.postMessage){
     $(window).bind("message",function(event){
       $("#to").val(event.originalEvent.data);
     });
➤ }else{
➤     $.getScript("javascripts/jquery.postmessage.js", function(){
➤       $.receiveMessage(
➤         function(event){
➤           $("#to").val(event.data);
➤         });
➤
➤     });
➤ }
```

That's it! We can now talk across windows in a whole bunch of browsers. This is just the beginning, though; you can expand this technique to do two-way communication, too. Any window can be a sender or a receiver, so take a look at the specification and see what you can build!

Tip 25

Chatting with Web Sockets

Real-time interaction has been something web developers have been trying to do for many years, but most of the implementations have involved using JavaScript to periodically hit the remote server to check for changes. HTTP is a stateless protocol, so a web browser makes a connection to a server, gets a response, and disconnects. Doing any kind of real-time work over a stateless protocol can be quite rough. The HTML5 specification introduced Web Sockets, which let the browser make a stateful connection to a remote server.[7] We can use Web Sockets to build all kinds of great applications. One of the best ways to get a feel for how Web Sockets work is to write a chat client, which, coincidentally, AwesomeCo wants for its support site.

AwesomeCo wants to create a simple web-based chat interface on its support site that will let members of the support staff communicate internally, because the support staff is located in different cities. We'll use Web Sockets to implement the web interface for the chat server. Users can connect and send a message to the server. Every connected user will see the message. Our visitors can assign themselves a nickname by sending a message such as "/nick brian," mimicking the IRC chat protocol. We won't be writing the actual server for this, because that has thankfully already been written by another developer.[8]

The Chat Interface

We're looking to build a very simple chat interface that looks like Figure 29, *Our chat interface*, on page 191, with a form to change the user's nickname, a large area where the messages will appear, and, finally, a form to post a message to the chat.

In a new HTML5 page, we'll add the markup for the chat interface, which consists of two forms and a div that will contain the chat messages.

---

7. Web Sockets have been spun off into their own specification, which you can find at http://www.w3.org/TR/websockets/.
8. Take a look at *Servers*, on page 196 for more about the servers.

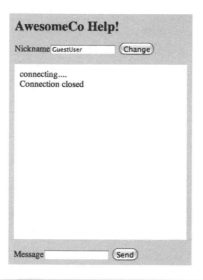

Figure 29—Our chat interface

`html5_websockets/public/index.html`

```html
<div id="chat_wrapper">
  <h2>AwesomeCo Help!</h2>
  <form id="nick_form" action="#" method="post" accept-charset="utf-8">
    <p>
      <label>Nickname
        <input id="nickname" type="text" value="GuestUser"/>
      </label>
      <input type="submit" value="Change">
    </p>
  </form>

  <div id="chat">connecting....</div>

  <form id="chat_form" action="#" method="post" accept-charset="utf-8">
    <p>
      <label>Message
        <input id="message" type="text" />
      </label>
      <input type="submit" value="Send">
    </p>
  </form>
</div>
```

We'll also need to add links to a style sheet and a JavaScript file that will contain our code to communicate with our Web Sockets server.

html5_websockets/public/index.html

```
<script src='chat.js' type='text/javascript'></script>
<link rel="stylesheet" href="style.css" media="screen">
```

Our style sheet contains these style definitions:

html5_websockets/public/style.css

```
Line 1  #chat_wrapper{
          width: 320px;
          height: 440px;
          background-color: #ddd;
     5    padding: 10px;
        }

        #chat_wrapper h2{
          margin: 0;
    10  }

        #chat{
          width: 300px;
          height: 300px;
    15    overflow: auto;
          background-color: #fff;
          padding: 10px;
        }
```

On line 15, we set the overflow property on the chat message area so that its height is fixed and any text that doesn't fit should be hidden, viewable with scrollbars.

With our interface in place, we can get to work on the JavaScript that will make it talk with our chat server.

Talking to the Server

No matter what Web Sockets server we're working with, we'll use the same pattern over and over. We'll make a connection to the server, and then we'll listen for events from the server and respond appropriately.

Event	Description
onopen()	Fires when the connection with the server has been established
onmessage()	Fires when the connection with the server sends a message
onclose()	Fires when the connection with the server has been lost or closed

In our chat.js file, we first need to connect to our Web Sockets server, like this:

```
html5_websockets/public/chat.js
var webSocket = new WebSocket('ws://localhost:9394/');
```

When we connect to the server, we should let the user know. We define the onopen() method like this:

```
html5_websockets/public/chat.js
webSocket.onopen = function(event){
  $('#chat').append('<br>Connected to the server');
};
```

When the browser opens the connection to the server, we put a message in the chat window. Next, we need to display the messages sent to the chat server. We do that by defining the onmessage() method like this:

```
html5_websockets/public/chat.js
webSocket.onmessage = function(event){
  $('#chat').append("<br>" + event.data);
  $('#chat').animate({scrollTop: $('#chat').height()});
};
```

The message comes back to us via the event object's data property. We just add it to our chat window. We'll prepend a break so each response falls on its own line, but you could mark this up any way you wanted.

Next we'll handle disconnections. The onclose() method fires whenever the connection is closed.

```
html5_websockets/public/chat.js
webSocket.onclose = function(event){
  $("#chat").append('<br>Connection closed');
};
```

Now we just need to hook up the text area for the chat form so we can send our messages to the chat server.

```
html5_websockets/public/chat.js
$(function(){
  $("form#chat_form").submit(function(e){
    e.preventDefault();
    var textfield = $("#message");
    webSocket.send(textfield.val());
    textfield.val("");
  });
})
```

We hook into the form submit event, grab the value of the form field, and send it to the chat server using the send() method.

We implement the nickname-changing feature the same way, except we prefix the message we're sending with "/nick." The chat server will see that and change the user's name.

html5_websockets/public/chat.js

```
$("form#nick_form").submit(function(e){
  e.preventDefault();
  var textfield = $("#nickname");
  webSocket.send("/nick " + textfield.val());
});
```

That's all there is to it. Safari 5 and Chrome 5 users can immediately participate in real-time chats using this client. Of course, we still need to support browsers without native Web Sockets support. We'll do that using Flash.

Falling Back

Browsers may not all have support for making socket connections, but Adobe Flash has had it for quite some time. We can use Flash to act as our socket communication layer, and thanks to the web-socket-js[9] library, implementing a Flash fallback is a piece of cake.

We can download a copy of the plug-in[10] and place it within our project. We then need to include the three JavaScript files on our page:

html5_websockets/public/index.html

```
<script type="text/javascript" src="websocket_js/swfobject.js"></script>
<script type="text/javascript" src="websocket_js/FABridge.js"></script>
<script type="text/javascript" src="websocket_js/web_socket.js"></script>

<script src='chat.js' type='text/javascript'></script>
<link rel="stylesheet" href="style.css" media="screen">

</head>
<body>
<div id="chat_wrapper">
  <h2>AwesomeCo Help!</h2>
  <form id="nick_form" action="#" method="post" accept-charset="utf-8">
    <p>
      <label>Nickname
        <input id="nickname" type="text" value="GuestUser"/>
      </label>
      <input type="submit" value="Change">
    </p>
  </form>
```

---

9. http://github.com/gimite/web-socket-js/
10. http://github.com/gimite/web-socket-js/archives/master

```
<div id="chat">connecting....</div>

<form id="chat_form" action="#" method="post" accept-charset="utf-8">
  <p>
    <label>Message
      <input id="message" type="text" />
    </label>
    <input type="submit" value="Send">
  </p>
</form>
</div>

</body>
</html>
```

The only change we need to make to our chat.js file is to set a variable that specifies the location of the WebSocketMain file.

html5_websockets/public/chat.js
```
WEB_SOCKET_SWF_LOCATION = "websocket_js/WebSocketMain.swf";
```

With that in place, our chat application will work on all major browsers, provided that the server hosting your chat server also serves a Flash Socket Policy file.

Flash Socket Policy What?

For security purposes, Flash Player will only communicate via sockets with servers that allow connections to Flash Player. Flash Player attempts to retrieve a Flash Socket Policy file first on port 843 and then on the same port your server uses. It will expect the server to return a response like this:

```
<cross-domain-policy>
    <allow-access-from domain="*" to-ports="*" />
</cross-domain-policy>
```

This is a very generic policy file that allows everyone to connect to this service. You'd want to specify the policy to be more restrictive if you were working with more sensitive data. Just remember that you have to serve this file from the same server that's serving your Web Sockets server, on either the same port or the port 843.

The example code for this section contains a simple Flash Socket Policy server written in Ruby that you can use for testing. See *Servers*, on page 196, for more on how to set that up on your own environment for testing.

Chat servers are just the beginning. With Web Sockets, we now have a robust and simple way to push data to our visitors' browsers.

Servers

The book's source code distribution contains a version of the Web Sockets server we're targeting. It's written in Ruby, so you'll need a Ruby interpreter. For instructions on getting Ruby working on your system, see the file RUBY_README.txt within the book's source code files.

You can start it up by navigating to its containing folder and typing this:

```
ruby server.rb
```

In addition to the chat server, there are two other servers you may want to use while testing the examples in this chapter. The first server, client.rb, serves the chat interface and JavaScript files. The other server, flashpolicyserver, serves a Flash Policy file that our Flash-based Web Sockets fallback code will need to contact in order to connect to the actual chat server. Flash Player uses these policy files to determine whether it is allowed to talk to a remote domain.

If you're running on a Mac or a Linux-based operating system, you can start all these servers at once with this:

```
rake start
```

from the html5_websockets folder.

Tip 26

Finding Yourself: Geolocation

Geolocation is a technique for discovering where people are, based on their computer's location. Of course, "computer" really can mean smart phone, tablet, or other portable device as well as a desktop computer. Geolocation determines a person's whereabouts by looking at their computer's IP address, MAC address, Wi-Fi hotspot location, or even GPS coordinates if available. Although not strictly part of HTML5 the specification, Geolocation is often associated with HTML5 because it's coming on the scene at the same time. Unlike Web Storage, Geolocation was never part of the HTML5 specification. Like Web Storage, it's a very useful technology that is already implemented in Firefox, Safari, and Chrome. Let's see how we can use it.

Locating Awesomeness

We've been asked to create a contact page for the AwesomeCo website, and the CIO has asked whether we could show people's location on a map along with the various AwesomeCo support centers. He'd love to see a prototype, so we'll get one up and running quickly.

We'll use Google's Static Map API for this because it doesn't require an API key and we're just going to generate a very simple map.

AwesomeCo service centers are located in Portland, Oregon; Chicago, Illinois; and Providence, Rhode Island. Google's Static Map API makes it really easy to plot these points on a map. All we have to do is construct an img tag and pass the addresses in the URL, like this:

html5geo/index.html
```
<img id="map" alt="Map of AwesomeCo Service Center locations"
src="http://maps.google.com/maps/api/staticmap?
&size=900x300
&sensor=false
&maptype=roadmap
&markers=color:green|label:A|1+Davol+square,+Providence,+RI+02906-3810
&markers=color:green|label:B|22+Southwest+3rd+Avenue,Portland,+OR
&markers=color:green|label:C|77+West+Wacker+Drive+Chicago+IL">
```

We define the size of the image, and then we tell the Maps API that we did not use any sensor device, such as a GPS or client-side geolocation with the information we're passing to this map. Then we define each marker on the map by giving it a label and the address. We could use a comma-separated pair of coordinates for these markers if we had them, but this is easier for our demonstration.

How to Be Found

We need to plot our visitor's current location on this map, and we'll do that by providing another marker on the map by using our latitude and longitude for a new marker. We can ask the browser to grab our visitor's latitude and longitude, like this:

```
html5geo/index.html
navigator.geolocation.getCurrentPosition(function(position) {
  showLocation(position.coords.latitude, position.coords.longitude);
});
```

This method prompts the user to provide us with their coordinates. If the visitor allows us to use their location information, we call the showLocation() method.

The showLocation() method takes the latitude and longitude and reconstructs the image, replacing the existing image source with the new one. Here's how we implement that method:

```
html5geo/index.html
Line 1  var showLocation = function(lat, lng){
     2    var fragment = "&markers=color:red|color:red|label:Y|" + lat + "," + lng;
     3    var image = $("#map");
     4    var source = image.attr("src") + fragment;
     5    source = source.replace("sensor=false", "sensor=true");
     6    image.attr("src", source);
     7  };
```

Rather than duplicate the entire image source code, we'll append our location's latitude and longitude to the existing image's source.

Before we assign the modified image source back to the document, we need to change the sensor parameter from false to true. We'll do that on line 5 with the replace() method.

When we bring it up in our browser, we'll see our location, marked with a "Y" among the other locations. To see an example, take a look at Figure 30, *Our current location is marked on the map with a Y.*, on page 199.

Figure 30—Our current location is marked on the map with a Y.

Falling Back

As it stands, visitors to the page will still see the map with the locations of the AwesomeCo support centers, but we will get a JavaScript error if we try to load our page. We need to detect support for geolocation before we attempt to get the visitor's location, like this:

html5geo/index.html
```
if (navigator.geolocation) {
  navigator.geolocation.getCurrentPosition(function(position) {
    showLocation(position.coords.latitude, position.coords.longitude);
  });
}else{
};
```

Google's Ajax API[11] does location lookup, so it's a great fallback solution. You will need to obtain an API key to use this on your site when you go live, but you don't need one to try this locally.[12]

Our fallback looks like this:

html5geo/index.html
```
Line 1  var key = "your_key";
        var script = "http://www.google.com/jsapi?key=" + key;
        $.getScript(script, function(){
```

---

11. http://code.google.com/apis/ajax/documentation/#ClientLocation
12. You will need a key if you host via http://localhost/ too. You can get one at
    http://code.google.com/apis/ajaxsearch/signup.html.

```
   if ((typeof google == 'object') &&
5     google.loader && google.loader.ClientLocation) {
        showLocation(google.loader.ClientLocation.latitude,
                  google.loader.ClientLocation.longitude);
     }else{
       var message = $("<p>Couldn't find your address.</p>");
10     message.insertAfter("#map");
     };
});
```

We're using jQuery's getScript() method to load the Google Ajax API. We then use Google's ClientLocation() method on line 5 to get a visitor's location and invoke our showLocation() method to plot the location on our map.

Unfortunately, Google can't geolocate every IP address out there, so we may still not be able to plot the user on our map; therefore, we account for that by placing a message underneath our image on line 9. Our fallback solution isn't foolproof, but it does give us a greater chance of locating our visitor.

Without a reliable method of getting coordinates from the client, we'll just need to provide a way for the user to provide us with an address, but that's an exercise I'll leave up to you.

10.1 The Future

The techniques we talked about in this chapter, although not all part of HTML5 proper, represent the future of web development. We'll be pushing many more things to the client side. Better history management will make Ajax and client-side applications much more intuitive. Web Sockets can replace periodic polling of remote services for the display of real-time data. Cross-document Messaging lets us merge web applications that usually would never be able to interact, and Geolocation will eventually let us build better location-aware web applications, which become more and more relevant every day with the growing mobile computing market.

Explore these APIs and keep an eye on their adoption. You may soon find these to be invaluable tools in your web development toolbox.

CHAPTER 11

Where to Go Next

Most of this book focuses on things you can do right now, but there are some other things you will be able to start using very soon that will make standards-based web development even more interesting, from 3D canvas support with WebGL to new storage APIs, CSS3 transitions, and native drag-and-drop support. This chapter discusses some of the things on the horizon, so you can get an idea of what to expect. We'll talk about things that you may be able to use in at least one browser but don't have good enough fallback solutions or are too far undefined to start working with right now:[1]

CSS3 transitions
> Animations on interaction. *[C3, S3.2, F4, O10.5, IOS3.2, A2]*

Web Workers
> Background processing for JavaScript. *[C3, S4, F3.5, O10.6]*

3D canvas with WebGL.[2]
> Creating 3D objects on the canvas. *[C5, F4]*

IndexedDB
> Advanced client-side key/value database storage similar to NoSQL solutions. *[F4]*

Drag and Drop
> API for drag-and-drop interaction. *[C3, S4, F3.5, IE6, A2]*

---

1. In the descriptions that follow, browser support is shown in square brackets using a shorthand code and the minimum supported version number. The codes used are *C:* Google Chrome, *F:* Firefox, *IE:* Internet Explorer, *O:* Opera, *S:* Safari, *IOS:* iOS devices with Mobile Safari, and *A:* Android Browser.
2. Disabled by default in supported browsers at the time of writing

Form validation

Client-side validation of inputs. *[C5, S5, 10.6]*

We'll start by looking at CSS3 transitions and how we can use them in WebKit browsers.

11.1 CSS3 Transitions

Interaction invitations are important to good user experience design, and CSS has supported the :hover pseudoclass for some time so that we can do some basic interaction cues on our elements. Here's some CSS markup that styles a link so it looks like a button:

css3transitions/style.css
```
a.button{
  padding: 10px;
  border: 1px solid #000;
  text-decoration: none;
}

a.button:hover{
 background-color: #bbb;
 color: #fff
}
```

When we place our cursor over the button, the background changes from white to gray, and the text changes from black to white. It's an instant transition. CSS3 transitions[3] let us do quite a bit more than this, including simple animations that were possible only with JavaScript. For example, we can make this transition into a cross-fade by adding the following highlighted code to the style definition:

css3transitions/style.css
```
Line 1  a.button{
          padding: 10px;
          border: 1px solid #000;
          text-decoration: none;
     5    -webkit-transition-property: background-color, color;
          -webkit-transition-duration: 1s;
          -webkit-transition-timing-function: ease-out;
        }

    10  a.button:hover{
         background-color: #bbb;
         color: #fff
        }
```

---

3.   http://dev.w3.org/csswg/css3-transitions/

On line 5, we specify what properties get the transition applied. In this case, we're changing the background and foreground colors. We specify the duration of the animation on line 6, and we specify the transition's timing function on line 7.

Timing Functions

The transition-timing-function property describes how transitions happen over time in relation to the duration you've set. We specify this timing function using a cubic Bezier curve, which is defined by four control points on a graph. Each point has an X value and a Y value, from 0 to 1. The first and last control points are always set to (0.0,0.0) and (1.0,1.0), and the two middle points determine the shape of the curve.

A linear curve has its control points set to the two end points, which creates a straight line at a 45-degree angle. The four points for a linear curve are ((0.0, 0.0), (0.0,0.0), (1.0, 1.0), (1.0, 1.0)), and it looks like this:

A more complex curve, with points ((0.0, 0.0), (0.42,0.0), (1.0, 1.0), (1.0, 1.0)), called an *ease-in* curve, looks like this:

This time, only the second point has changed, which is what causes the bottom-left part of the line to curve.

Even more complex is the ease-in-out curve, which has a curve at the bottom and at the top, like this:

The points for this curve are ((0.0, 0.0), (0.42,0.0), (0.58, 1.0), (1.0, 1.0)).

We can specify these points right in the CSS property, or we can use some predefined ones like we did in our example.

Our choices are default, ease-in, ease-out, ease-in-out, ease-out-in, and cubic-bezier, in which you set the points of the curve yourself.

If you want the rate to be constant, you'd use linear. If you want the animation to start slow and speed up, you'd use ease-in. If you want to learn a little more about making these curves, there's a great public domain script[4] that shows you examples and helps you see the coordinates.

Play around with transitions, but keep in mind that you want your interface to be usable first and pretty second. Don't build transitions that frustrate the user, such as things that flicker or take too long to animate. You may also want to investigate CSS3 animations,[5] another method for changing CSS properties over time.

11.2 Web Workers

Web Workers[6] are not part of the HTML5 specification, but you may find them useful if you need to do some background processing on the client side, so they're worth mentioning.

We use JavaScript for all of our client-side coding, but JavaScript is a single-threaded language—only one thing can happen at a time. If a task takes a long time, we force the user to wait until the task has finished. Web Workers solve this problem by creating a simple way to write concurrent programs.

If we have a script called worker.js that does some image processing, we can invoke it like this:

webworkers/application.js
```
var worker = new Worker("worker.js");
```

Any JavaScript file can be launched as a worker, but in order for the worker to be independent, your worker script can't access the DOM. That means you can't manipulate elements directly.

Our main script can send messages to the worker script using postMessage() like this:

---

4. http://www.netzgesta.de/dev/cubic-bezier-timing-function.html
5. http://www.w3.org/TR/css3-animations/
6. http://www.whatwg.org/specs/web-workers/current-work/

```
webworkers/application.js
$("#button").click(function(event){
  $("#output").html("starting...");
  worker.postMessage("start");
});
```

Our worker script can then send messages back to the main page, also using the postmessage() method.

```
webworkers/worker.js
onmessage = function(event) {
  if(event.data === "start"){
    // this loop counts. Do something awesome instead.
    for (var x = 1; x <= 100000; x++){
      postMessage(x);
    }
  }
};
```

We respond to those events by listening to the onmessage event in our main script. Every time the worker posts back, this code will fire:

```
webworkers/application.js
worker.onmessage = function(event){
  $("#output").html(event.data);
}
```

This API works just like the API for cross domain messaging, which we talked about in Tip 24, *Talking Across Domains*, on page 183. There's no support for Web Workers in Internet Explorer, so you'd need to rely on Google Chrome Frame, but if you're looking to do some heavier nonblocking client-side work, you'll want to look into this further.

11.3 Native Drag-and-Drop Support

Letting users drag and drop interface elements is something we've been able to do with JavaScript libraries for quite a while, but the W3C has adopted Microsoft's Drag and Drop implementation as part of the HTML5 specification.[7] It's supported by Firefox, Safari, Internet Explorer, and Chrome, but in actuality it's a mess.

The implementation at first appears to be straightforward; we designate an element as "draggable," we then designate an element that watches for a dropped object, and we execute some code when that happens.

---

7.   http://dev.w3.org/html5/spec/dnd.html#dnd

In reality, it's not nearly that simple. To demonstrate, let's create a simple drag-and-drop interface that lets us drag small images into a drop area that will load the larger version.

html5drag/index.html
```html
<div id="images">
  <img src="images/red_thumb.jpg"
      data-large="images/red.jpg" alt="A red flower">
  <img src="images/purple_thumb.jpg"
      data-large="images/purple.jpg" alt="A white and purple flower">
  <img src="images/white_thumb.jpg"
      data-large="images/white.jpg" alt="A white flower">

</div>

<div id="preview">
  <p>Drop images here</p>
</div>
```

We're using custom data attributes here to hold the source of the larger version of our photos.

Next we'll add some basic styles to float the two columns:

html5drag/style.css
```css
#images img{
  -webkit-user-drag
}

#images{
  float: left;
  width: 240px;
  margin-right: 10px;
}

#preview{
  float: left;
  width: 500px;
  background-color: #ddd;
  height: 335px;
}

.hover{
  border: 10px solid #000;
  background-color: #bbb !important;
}
```

At this point, our interface looks like the one in Figure 31, *Our photo viewer*, on page 207. Now let's add some events so we can drag the photos.

Drop images here

Figure 31—Our photo viewer

Drag-and-Drop Events

We'll need to work with several events related to dragging and dropping elements.

Event	Description
ondragstart	Fires when the user starts dragging the object
ondragend	Fires when the user stops dragging the object *for any reason*
ondragenter	Fires when a draggable element is moved into a drop listener
ondragover	Fires when the user drags an element over a drop listener
ondragleave	Fires when the user drags an element out of drop listener
ondrop	Fires when the user drops an element into a drop listener successfully
ondrag	Fires when the user drags an element anywhere; fires constantly but can give X and Y coordinates of the mouse cursor

That's a total of seven events just to handle dragging and dropping elements, and some of the events have default behaviors. If we don't override them, the whole thing fails.

First, we need to define all of our list items as draggable.

```
html5drag/application.js
var contacts = $('#images img');
contacts.attr('draggable', 'true');
```

We're adding the draggable HTML5 attribute. We could do this in our markup, but since we require JavaScript to do the interaction, we'll apply this attribute with our script.

When we drag the image, we want to grab the address of the large image and store it. We'll bind to the ondragstart event, and to keep it simple and cross-platform, we'll use jQuery's bind() method.[8]

```
html5drag/application.js
Line 1  contacts.bind('dragstart', function(event) {
     2      var data = event.originalEvent.dataTransfer;
     3      var src = $(this).attr("data-large");
     4      data.setData("Text", src);
     5      return true;
     6  });
```

The specification provides a dataStorage mechanism that lets us specify the type of data and the data itself, which is passed along as part of the event. jQuery's bind() method wraps the event in its own object, so we use the originalevent property on 2 to access the real event. We store the URL to the image on the event by using the setData() method on line 4, using Text as the data type.

Now that we can drag elements, let's talk about how we fire events when the user drops the elements.

Dropping Elements

We want our "To" form field to act as our drop target, so we'll locate it and bind the drop event.

```
html5drag/application.js
Line 1  var target = $('#preview');

        target.bind('drop', function(event) {
          var data = event.originalEvent.dataTransfer;
     5    var src = ( data.getData('Text') );

          var img = $("<img></img>").attr("src", src);
          $(this).html(img);
          if (event.preventDefault) event.preventDefault();
    10    return(false);
        });
```

---

8. Remember, we omit the on prefix for these events when we use that method.

We retrieve the image address we passed with the event using the getData() method on line 5, and we then create a new image element that we push into our content region.

We need to cancel the default ondrop event so it won't fire when our user drops the element onto the target. To do that, we need to use both preventdefault() and return false. Internet Explorer needs return false, and the other browsers need preventDefault().

If we try to use this in Chrome or Safari right now, it won't work quite right. At a minimum, we have to override the ondragover element. If we don't, our ondrag event won't respond. So, we'll do that by using this code:

html5drag/application.js
```
target.bind('dragover', function(event) {
  if (event.preventDefault) event.preventDefault();
  return false;
});
```

We're just canceling out the default event again the same way we did with the ondrop event. Let's do the same with the ondragend event too.

html5drag/application.js
```
contacts.bind('dragend', function(event) {
  if (event.preventDefault) event.preventDefault();
  return false;
});
```

This will cancel out any browser events that fire when our user stops dragging an element, but it won't interfere with our defined ondrop event.

Changing Styles

We want to let the user know they have dragged an element over a drop target, and we can do that using the ondragenter and ondragleave methods.

html5drag/application.js
```
target.bind('dragenter', function(event) {
  $(this).addClass('hover');
  if (event.preventDefault) event.preventDefault();
  return false;
});

target.bind('dragleave', function(event) {
  $(this).removeClass('hover');
  if (event.preventDefault) event.preventDefault();
  return false;
});
```

This applies our hover class in our style sheet, which will be applied and removed when these events fire.

File Dragging

Moving text and elements around the page is just the beginning. The specification allows developers to create interfaces that can receive files from the user's computer. Uploading a photo or attaching a file is as easy as dragging the file onto a specified target. In fact, Google's Gmail supports this if you are using Firefox 3.6 or Chrome 5.

If you want to explore this further, take a look at the excellent article[9] by Leslie Michael Orchard.

All Is Not Well

The behavior in various browsers is, to be kind, inconsistent. IE 8 works, but it breaks if we try to set the data type for setData() to Url instead of Text.

Additionally, in order to support dragging of elements that are not images or links in Safari 4, we'd need to add additional CSS to our style sheet.

```
#contents li{
  -webkit-user-drag
}
```

Throughout this book, we've discussed how important it is to keep style and behavior separated from content, and this flies right in the face of that concept.

Don't try dragging text onto form fields. Modern browsers already let you do this, but there's no good way to override that behavior.

As it stands, we can get much better results with much less code by using a JavaScript library that supports dragging and dropping like jQuery UI.[10]

Even with a library, we still have one last thing to worry about: accessibility. The specification doesn't say anything about how to handle users who can't use a mouse. If we implemented drag-and-drop functionality on our interfaces, we'd need to develop a secondary method that didn't require JavaScript or a mouse to work, and that method would depend on what we're trying to do.

This specification has a lot of potential, but it also has some things that need to be addressed. Use it if it makes sense, but ensure you don't force your users into something they can't use.

---

9.   http://decafbad.com/blog/2009/07/15/html5-drag-and-drop
10.   http://docs.jquery.com/UI/Draggable

11.4 WebGL

We talked about the canvas element's 2D context in this book, but there's another specification in progress that describes how to work with 3D objects. The WebGL[11] specification isn't part of HTML5, but Apple, Google, Opera, and Mozilla are part of the working group and have implemented some support in their browsers.

Working with 3D graphics is well beyond the scope of this book, but the site Learning WebGL[12] has some great examples and tutorials.

11.5 Indexed Database API

In this book, we talked about two methods for storing data on the client: Web Storage and Web SQL Storage. The Mozilla foundation took issue with the Web SQL specification, stating that they didn't think it was a good idea to base the specification on a specific SQL engine. They introduced a new specification called the Indexed Database API, which is scheduled to become a standard of its own.[13]

The Indexed Database API is a key/value store similar to the Web Storage APIs like localStorage and sessionStorage, but it provides methods for performing advanced queries. Unfortunately, at the time of writing, there are no implementations of this specification available, so it's not even worth going into any implementation details because they will most likely change between now and the time it's implemented. Firefox 4 and Chrome 7 are expected to include support.

This is the specification you'll want to watch closely, because Web SQL is at an impasse, and Mozilla has stated numerous times that it has no plans to ever implement Web SQL in Firefox, because Mozilla is uncomfortable with the SQL dialect and doesn't think that the specification should be based on one particular database implementation. The Web SQL specification uses the SQLite database dialect, which could change independent of the specification. It's very likely that Internet Explorer will implement this specification as well, because Microsoft has taken an interest in its development.[14]

---

11. https://cvs.khronos.org/svn/repos/registry/trunk/public/webgl/doc/spec/WebGL-spec.html
12. http://learningwebgl.com/blog/?p=11
13. http://www.w3.org/TR/IndexedDB/
14. http://hacks.mozilla.org/2010/06/beyond-html5-database-apis-and-the-road-to-indexeddb/

11.6 Client-Side Form Validation

The HTML5 specification lists several attributes we can use to validate user input on the client side, so we can catch simple input errors before the user sends the requests to the server. We've been able to do this for years using JavaScript, but HTML5 forms can use new attributes to specify the behavior.

We can ensure that a user has required a form field by adding the required attribute like this:

html5validation/index.html
```
<label for="name">Name</label>
<input type="text" name="name" autofocus required id="name">
```

Browsers can then prevent the form from submitting and display a nice error message, and we don't have to write a single line of JavaScript validation. Opera does this right now, as you can see in Figure 32, *Opera displays a highlighted warning.*, on page 213.

This lets users fail early, without waiting for a server response to find out whether they made a mistake. This behavior could be disabled or unavailable or just simply not correctly implemented, so you still need to make sure you have a server-side strategy for validating data. It's definitely something to start thinking about now, though, because you can then easily locate the required fields and style the interface with CSS so that the required fields stand out from the rest.

You can take this one step further with the pattern attribute, which lets you specify a regular expression to ensure that the content meets your criteria.

html5validation/index.html
```
<input type="text"
       name="acctnumber" id="acctnumber"
       required
       pattern="^[1-9]+[0-9]*$">
```

Although no current browser uses this through the user interface, using this markup as the basis for a JavaScript validation library would be easy to implement.

11.7 Onward!

It's an exciting time to be a developer. This book just barely scrapes the surface of what the future holds for web developers. There's so much more to the specifications, and I encourage you to dig deeper. I hope you take the things you learned here and continue to build and explore, watching the various specifications as you do so.

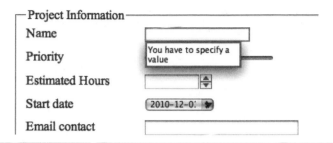

Figure 32—Opera displays a highlighted warning.

Now go build something awesome!

Features Quick Reference

In the descriptions that follow, browser support is shown in square brackets using a shorthand code and the minimum supported version number. The codes used are *C:* Google Chrome, *F:* Firefox, *IE:* Internet Explorer, *O:* Opera, *S:* Safari, *IOS:* iOS devices with Mobile Safari, and *A:* Android Browser.

A1.1 New Elements

Referenced in Tip 1, *Redefining a Blog Using Semantic Markup*, on page 14

`<header>`
> Defines a header region of a page or section. *[C5, F3.6, IE8, S4, O10]*

`<footer>`
> Defines a footer region of a page or section. *[C5, F3.6, IE8, S4, O10]*

`<nav>`
> Defines a navigation region of a page or section. *[C5, F3.6, IE8, S4, O10]*

`<section>`
> Defines a logical region of a page or a grouping of content. *[C5, F3.6, IE8, S4, O10]*

`<article>`
> Defines an article or complete piece of content. *[C5, F3.6, IE8, S4, O10]*

`<aside>`
> Defines secondary or related content. *[C5, F3.6, IE8, S4, O10]*

`<meter>`
> Describes an amount within a range. *[C5, F3.5, S4, O10]*

<progress>

Control that shows real-time progress toward a goal. *[Unsupported at publication time.]*.

A1.2 Attributes

Custom data attributes

Allows the addition of custom attributes to any elements using the data-pattern. *[All browsers support reading these via JavaScript's getAttribute() method.]*

Referenced in Tip 2, *Creating Pop-up Windows with Custom Data Attributes*, on page 26

In-place editing support [<p contenteditable>lorem ipsum</p>]

Support for in-place editing of content via the browser. *[C4, S3.2, IE6, O10.1]*

Referenced in Tip 6, *In-Place Editing with contenteditable*, on page 48

A1.3 Forms

Referenced in Tip 3, *Describing Data with New Input Fields*, on page 33

Email field [<input type="email">]

Displays a form field for email addresses. *[O10.1, IOS]*

URL field [<input type="url">]

Displays a form field for URLs. *[O10.1, IOS]*

Telephone field [<input type="tel">]

Displays a form field for telephone numbers. *[O10.1, IOS]*

Search field [<input type="search">]

Displays a form field for search keywords. *[C5, S4, O10.1, IOS]*

Slider (range) [<input type="range">]

Displays a slider control. *[C5, S4, O10.1]*

Number [<input type="number">]

Displays a form field for numbers, often as a spinbox. *[C5, S5, O10.1, IOS]*

Date fields [<input type="date">]

Displays a form field for dates. Supports date, month, or week. *[C5, S5, O10.1]*

Dates with Times [<input type="datetime">]

> Displays a form field for dates with times. Supports datetime, datetime-local, or time. *[C5, S5, O10.1]*

Color [<input type="color">]

> Displays a field for specifying colors. *[C5, S5]* (Chrome 5 and Safari 5 understand the Color field but do not display any specific control.)

A1.4 Form Field Attributes

Autofocus support [<input type="text" autofocus>]

> Support for placing the focus on a specific form element. *[C5, S4]*

> Referenced in Tip 4, *Jumping to the First Field with Autofocus*, on page 40

Placeholder support [<input type="email" placeholder="me@example.com">]

> Support for displaying placeholder text inside of a form field. *[C5, S4, F4]*

> Referenced in Tip 5, *Providing Hints with Placeholder Text*, on page 41

required [<input type="email" required >]

> Makes a field required. *[C5, S5, O10.6]*

> Referenced in Section 11.6, *Client-Side Form Validation*, on page 212

pattern [<input type="text" pattern="^[1-9]+[0-9]*$">]

> Validates form field data to match the specified regular expression pattern. *[C5, S5, O10.6]*

> Referenced in Section 11.6, *Client-Side Form Validation*, on page 212

A1.5 Accessibility

The role attribute [<div role="document">]

> Identifies responsibility of an element to screen readers. *[C3, F3.6, S4, IE8, O9.6]*

> Referenced in Tip 11, *Providing Navigation Hints with ARIA Roles*, on page 81

aria-live [<div aria-live="polite">]

> Identifies a region that updates automatically, possibly by Ajax. *[F3.6 (Windows), S4, IE8]*

> Referenced in Tip 12, *Creating an Accessible Updatable Region*, on page 86

aria-atomic [<div aria-live="polite" aria-atomic="true">]

Identifies whether the entire content of a live region should be read or just the elements that changed. *[F3.6 (Windows), S4, IE8]*

Referenced in Tip 12, *Creating an Accessible Updatable Region*, on page 86

A1.6 Multimedia

<canvas> [<canvas><p>Alternative content</p></canvas>]

Supports creation of vector-based graphics via JavaScript. *[C4, F3, IE9, S3.2, O10.1, IOS3.2, A2]*

Referenced in Chapter 6, *Drawing on the Canvas*, on page 93

<audio> [<audio src="drums.mp3"></audio>]

Play audio natively in the browser. *[C4, F3.6, IE9, S3.2, O10.1, IOS3, A2]*

Referenced in Tip 15, *Working with Audio*, on page 115

<video> [<video src="tutorial.m4v"></video>]

Play video natively in the browser. *[C4, F3.6, IE9, S3.2, O10.5, IOS3, A2]*

Referenced in Tip 16, *Embedding Video*, on page 119

A1.7 CSS3

Referenced in Section 11.1, *CSS3 Transitions*, on page 202

:nth-of-type [p:nth-of-type(2n+1){color: red;}]

Finds all n elements of a certain type. *[C2, F3.5, S3, IE9, O9.5, IOS]*

Referenced in Tip 7, *Styling Tables with Pseudoclasses*, on page 57

:first-child [p:first-child{color:blue;}]

Finds the first child element. *[C2, F3.5, S3, IE9, O9.5, IOS3, A2]*

Referenced in Tip 7, *Styling Tables with Pseudoclasses*, on page 57

:nth-child [p:nth-child(2n+1){color: red;}]

Finds a specific child element counting forward. *[C2, F3.5, S3, IE9, O9.5, IOS3, A2]*

Referenced in Tip 7, *Styling Tables with Pseudoclasses*, on page 57

:last-child [p:last-child{color:blue;}]

Finds the last child element. *[C2, F3.5, S3, IE9, O9.5, IOS3, A2]*

Referenced in Tip 7, *Styling Tables with Pseudoclasses*, on page 57

:nth-last-child [p:nth-last-child(2){color: red;}]

Finds a specific child element counting backward. *[C2, F3.5, S3, IE9, O9.5, IOS3, A2]*

Referenced in Tip 7, *Styling Tables with Pseudoclasses*, on page 57

:first-of-type [p:first-of-type{color:blue;}]

Finds the first element of the given type. *[C2, F3.5, S3, IE9, O9.5, IOS3, A2]*

Referenced in Tip 7, *Styling Tables with Pseudoclasses*, on page 57

:last-of-type [p:last-of-type{color:blue;}]

Finds the last element of the given type. *[C2, F3.5, S3, IE9, O9.5, IOS3, A2]*

Referenced in Tip 7, *Styling Tables with Pseudoclasses*, on page 57

Column support [#content{ column-count: 2; column-gap: 20px;
column-rule: 1px solid #ddccb5; }]

Divides a content area into multiple columns. *[C2, F3.5, S3, O9.5, IOS3, A2]*

Referenced in Tip 9, *Creating Multicolumn Layouts*, on page 70

:after [span.weight:after { content: "lbs"; color: #bbb; }]

Used with content to insert content after the specified element. *[C2, F3.5, S3, IE8, O9.5, IOS3, A2]*

Referenced in Tip 8, *Making Links Printable with :after and content*, on page 66

Media Queries [media="only all and (max-width: 480)"]

Apply styles based on device settings. *[C3, F3.5, S4, IE9, O10.1, IOS3, A2]*

Referenced in Tip 10, *Building Mobile Interfaces with Media Queries*, on page 76

border-radius [border-radius: 10px;]

Rounds corners of elements. *[C4, F3, IE9, S3.2, O10.5]*

Referenced in Tip 17, *Rounding Rough Edges*, on page 129

RGBa Supprt [background-color: rgba(255,0,0,0.5);]

Uses RGB color instead of hex codes along with transparency. *[C4, F3.5, IE9, S3.2, O10.1]*

Referenced in Tip 18, *Working with Shadows, Gradients, and Transformations*, on page 136 box-shadow [box-shadow: 10px 10px 5px #333;]

Creates drop shadows on elements. *[C3, F3.5, IE9, S3.2, O10.5]*

Referenced in Tip 18, *Working with Shadows, Gradients, and Transformations*, on page 136

Rotation: [transform: rotate(7.5deg);]

Rotates any element. *[C3, F3.5, IE9, S3.2, O10.5]*

Referenced in Tip 18, *Working with Shadows, Gradients, and Transformations*, on page 136

Gradients: [linear-gradient(top, #fff, #efefef);]

Creates gradients for use as images. *[C4, F3.5, S4]*

Referenced in Tip 18, *Working with Shadows, Gradients, and Transformations*, on page 136

@font-face [@font-face { font-family: AwesomeFont;
src: url(http://example.com/awesomeco.ttf); font-weight: bold; }]

Allows use of specific fonts via CSS. *[C4, F3.5, IE5+, S3.2, O10.1]*

Referenced in Tip 19, *Using Real Fonts*, on page 146

A1.8 Client-Side Storage

localStorage

Stores data in key/value pairs, tied to a domain, and persists across browser sessions. *[C5, F3.5, S4, IE8, O10.5, IOS, A]*

Referenced in Tip 20, *Saving Preferences with localStorage*, on page 158

sessionStorage

Stores data in key/value pairs, tied to a domain, and is erased when a browser session ends. *[C5, F3.5, S4, IE8, O10.5, IOS, A]*

Referenced in Tip 20, *Saving Preferences with localStorage*, on page 158

Web SQL Databases

Fully relational databases with support for creating tables, inserts, updates, deletes, and selects, with transactions. Tied to a domain and persists across sessions. *[C5, S3.2, O10.5, IOS3.2, A2]*

Referenced in Tip 21, *Storing Data in a Client-Side Relational Database*, on page 164

A1.9 Additional APIs

Offline Web Applications
> Defines files to be cached for offline use, allowing applications to run without an Internet connection. *[C4, S4, F3.5, O10.6, IOS3.2, A2]*

> Referenced in Tip 22, *Working Offline*, on page 175

History
> Manages the browser history. *[C5, S4, IE8, F3, O10.1 IOS3.2, A2]*

> Referenced in Tip 23, *Preserving History*, on page 180

Cross-document Messaging
> Sends messages between windows with content loaded on different domains. *[C5, S5, F4, IOS4.1, A2]*

> Referenced in Tip 24, *Talking Across Domains*, on page 183

Web Sockets
> Creates a stateful connection between a browser and a server. *[C5, S5, F4, IOS4.2]*

> Referenced in Tip 25, *Chatting with Web Sockets*, on page 190

Geolocation
> Gets latitude and longitude from the client's browser. *[C5, S5, F3.5, O10.6, IOS3.2, A2]*

> Referenced in Tip 26, *Finding Yourself: Geolocation*, on page 197

Web Workers
> Background processing for JavaScript. *[C3, S4, F3.5, O10.6]*

> Referenced in Section 11.2, *Web Workers*, on page 204

3D canvas with WebGL.[1]
> Creating 3D objects on the canvas. *[C5, F4]*

> Referenced in Section 11.4, *WebGL*, on page 211

Drag and Drop
> API for drag-and-drop interaction. *[C3, S4, F3.5, IE6, A2]*

> Referenced in Section 11.3, *Native Drag-and-Drop Support*, on page 205

---

1. Disabled by default in supported browsers at the time of writing

jQuery Primer

Writing JavaScript that works well across all major web browsers in a clean and concise way is a difficult chore. There are many libraries that make this process less painful, and jQuery is one of the most popular. It's easy to use, has a wide array of existing libraries, and is a good fit for easily creating fallback solutions.

This appendix introduces you to the parts of the jQuery library that we use elsewhere in the book. It's not meant to be a replacement for jQuery's excellent documentation,[1] nor is it going to be an exhaustive list of the features and methods available. It will, however, give you a good place to start.

A2.1 Loading jQuery

You can grab the jQuery library from the jQuery website[2] and link to the jQuery script directly, but we'll load jQuery from Google's servers, like this:

jquery/simple_selection.html

```
<script type="text/javascript"
  charset="utf-8"
  src="http://ajax.googleapis.com/ajax/libs/jquery/1.4.2/jquery.min.js">
</script>
```

Browsers can make only a few connections to a server at a time. If we distribute our images and scripts to multiple servers, our users can download our pages faster. Using Google's content delivery network has an additional benefit as well—since other sites link to the jQuery library at Google, our visitors may already have the library cached by their browser. As you probably already know, browsers use the full URL to a file to decide whether it has a

---

1. http://docs.jquery.com
2. http://www.jquery.com

cached copy. If you plan to work with jQuery on a laptop or on a computer without constant Internet access, you will want to link to a local copy instead.

A2.2 jQuery Basics

Once you have loaded the jQuery library on your page, you can start working with elements. jQuery has a function called the jQuery() function. This one function is the heart of the jQuery library. We use this function to fetch elements using CSS selectors and wrap them in jQuery objects so we can manipulate them. There's a shorter version of the jQuery() function, $();, and that's what we use in this book. Throughout the rest of this appendix, I'll refer to this function as "the jQuery function." Here's how it works:

If you wanted to find the h1 tag on a page, you'd use the following:

jquery/simple_selection.html
```
$("h1");
```

If you were looking for all elements with the class of important, you'd do this:

jquery/simple_selection.html
```
$(".important");
```

Take a look at that again. The only difference between those two examples is the CSS selector we used. The jQuery function returns a jQuery object, which is a special JavaScript object containing an array of the DOM elements that match the selector. This object has many useful predefined methods we can use to manipulate the elements we selected. Let's take a look at a few of those in detail.

A2.3 Methods to Modify Content

We use several jQuery methods to modify our HTML content as we work through this book.

Hide and Show

The hide() and show() methods make it easy to hide and show user interface elements. We can hide one or many elements on a page like this:

jquery/simple_selection.html
```
$("h1").hide();
```

To show them, we simply call the show() method instead. We use the hide() method throughout this book to hide page sections that only need to appear when JavaScript is disabled, such as transcripts or other fallback content.

html, val, and attr

We use the html()method to get and set the inner content of the specified element.

jquery/methods.html
```
$("#message").html("Hello World!");
```

Here, we're setting the content between the opening and closing h1 tags to "Hello World."

The val() method sets and retrieves the value from a form field. It works exactly like the html() method.

The attr() method lets us retrieve and set attributes on elements.

append, prepend, and wrap

The append() method adds a new child element after the existing elements. Given we have a simple form and an empty unordered list, like this:

jquery/methods.html
```
<form id="task_form">
  <label for="task">Task</label>
  <input type="text" id="task" >
  <input type="submit" value="Add">
</form>
<ul id="tasks">
</ul>
```

we can create new elements in the list by appending these new elements when we submit the form.

jquery/methods.html
```
$(function(){
  $("#task_form").submit(function(event){
    event.preventDefault();
    var new_element = $("<li>" + $("#task").val() + "</li>");
    $("#tasks").append(new_element);
  });
});
```

The prepend() method works the same way as the append() method but inserts the new element before any of the existing ones. The wrap() method wraps the selected element with the element represented by the jQuery object you specify.

jquery/methods.html
```
var wrapper = $("#message").wrap("<div class='wrapper'></div>").parent();
```

In this book, we create a few complex structures programmatically using these techniques.

CSS and Classes

We can use the css() method to define styles on elements, like this:

jquery/methods.html
```
$("label").css("color", "#f00");
```

We can define these one at a time, but we can also use a JavaScript hash to assign many CSS rules to the element:

jquery/methods.html
```
$("h1").css( {"color" : "red",
              "text-decoration" : "underline"}
          );
```

However, it's not a good idea to mix style with scripts. We can use jQuery's addClass() and removeClass() methods to add and remove classes when certain events occur. We can then associate styles with these classes. We can change the background on our form fields when they receive and lose focus by combining jQuery events and classes.

jquery/methods.html
```
$("input").focus(function(event){
  $(this).addClass("focused");
});

$("input").blur(function(event){
  $(this).removeClass("focused");
});
```

This is a trivial example that can be replaced by the :focus pseudoclass in CSS3 but that isn't supported in some browsers.

Chaining

Methods on jQuery objects return jQuery objects, which means we can chain methods indefinitely, like this:

jquery/simple_selection.html
```
$("h2").addClass("hidden").removeClass("visible");
```

You should take care not to abuse this, because this can make code harder to follow.

A2.4 Creating Elements

From time to time, we need to create new HTML elements so we can insert them into our document. We can use jQuery's jQuery() method to create these elements.

```
jquery/create_elements.html
var input = $("input");
```

Although we can use document.createElement("input"); to accomplish this, we can call additional methods easily if we use the jQuery function.

```
jquery/create_elements.html
var element = $("<p>Hello World</p>");
element.css("color", "#f00").insertAfter("#header");
```

This is another example where jQuery's chaining helps us build and manipulate structures quickly.

A2.5 Events

We often need to fire events when users interact with our page, and jQuery makes this very easy. In jQuery, many common events are simply methods on the jQuery object that take a function. For example, we can make all the links on a page with the class of popup open in a new window like this:

```
jquery/popup.html
Line 1 var links = $("a.popup");
   2 links.click(function(event){
   3   var address = $(this).attr('href');
   4   event.preventDefault();
   5   window.open(address);
   6 });
```

Inside our jQuery event handler, we can access the element we're working with by using the this keyword. On line 3, we pass this to the jQuery function so we can call the attr() method on it to quickly retrieve the link's destination address.

We use the preventDefault() function to keep the original event from firing so it doesn't interfere with what we're doing.

Bind

Some events aren't directly supported by jQuery, and we can use the bind() method to handle them. For example, when implementing the Drag and Drop part of the HTML5 specification, we need to cancel out the ondragover event. We use the bind() like this:

```
jquery/bind.html
target = $("#droparea")
target.bind('dragover', function(event) {
  if (event.preventDefault) event.preventDefault();
  return false;
});
```

Notice that we drop the on prefix for the event we're watching.

The Original Event

When we use any of the jQuery event functions like bind() or click(), jQuery wraps the JavaScript event in its own object and copies only *some* of the properties across. Sometimes we need to get to the actual event so we can access those properties that didn't get cloned. jQuery events give us access to the original event with the appropriately named originalEvent property. We can access the data property of the onmessage event like this:

```
$(window).bind("message", function(event){
  var message_data = event.originalEvent.data;
});
```

You can use this technique to call any of the original event's properties or methods.

A2.6 Document Ready

The phrase "unobtrusive JavaScript" refers to JavaScript that's kept completely separate from the content. Instead of adding onclick attributes to our HTML elements, we use event handlers like we just talked about in Section A2.5, *Events*, on page 227. We unobtrusively add behavior to our document, without modifying the document itself. Our HTML is not dependent on our users having JavaScript enabled.

One drawback to this method is that JavaScript can't "see" any of the elements in our document until they've been declared. We could include our JavaScript code in a script block at the bottom of the page after everything else has been rendered, but that isn't reusable across pages.

We could wrap our code in JavaScript's window.onLoad() event handler, but that event gets fired after all the content has loaded. This could cause a delay, meaning your users could be interacting with things before your events have been attached. We need a way to add our events when the DOM is loaded but before it's been displayed.

jQuery's document.ready function does exactly this, in a way that works across browsers. We use it like this:

jquery/ready.html
```
$(document).ready(function() {
  alert("Hi! L am a popup that displays when the page loads");
});
```

There's a shorter, more compact version that we'll be using throughout our code, which looks like this:

jquery/ready.html
```
$(function() {
  alert("Hi! L am a popup that displays when the page loads");
});
```

We use this pattern in almost every example in this book so that we can easily, unobtrusively add fallback solutions to our projects.

This is only a small sampling of what we can do with jQuery. Aside from the document manipulation features, jQuery provides methods for serializing forms and making Ajax requests and includes some utility functions that make looping and DOM traversal much easier. Once you become more comfortable with its use, you'll no doubt find many more ways to use it in your projects.

Encoding Audio and Video

Encoding audio and video for use with HTML5's audio and video tags is a complex subject that's out of scope for this book, but this short appendix will get you going in the right direction if you ever need to prepare your own content.

A3.1 Encoding Audio

You'll need to prepare your audio files in both MP3 and Vorbis formats to reach the widest possible audience, and to do that, you'll use a couple of tools.

For encoding MP3 files, Lame is going to give you the best quality. You'll want to use a variable bit rate when you encode. You can get a high-quality encode using something like this:

```
lame in.wav out.mp3 -V2 --vbr-new -q0 --lowpass 19.7
```

For Vorbis audio, you'll use Oggenc to encode the audio. To encode a good-sounding Vorbis file using a variable bitrate, you'd use something like this:

```
oggenc -q 3 inputfile.wav
```

Learn more about MP3 and Vorbis encoding at Hydrogen Audio.[1] The information there is excellent, but you'll need to experiment with settings that will work for you and your listeners.

A3.2 Encoding Video for the Web

You need to encode your video files to multiple formats if you want to reach every platform when using HTML5 video. Encoding to H.264, Theora, and VP8 can be a time-consuming practice, both in terms of setting up an open

---

1. Lame is at http://wiki.hydrogenaudio.org/index.php?title=Lame#Quick_start_.28short_answer.29 , and Vorbis is at http://wiki.hydrogenaudio.org/index.php?title=Recommended_Ogg_Vorbis.o

source encoders like FFMpeg[2] and actually running the encoding jobs. Encoding videos properly is beyond the scope of this book. We don't have enough pages to explain this command, which converts a file to VP8 using the WebM container:

```
ffmpeg -i blur.mov
        -f webm -vcodec libvpx_vp8 -acodec libvorbis
        -ab 160000 -sameq
        blur.webm
```

If you don't want to mess with the settings yourself, the web service Zencoder[3] can take your videos and encode them to all the formats necessary for use with HTML5 video. You place your video on Amazon S3 or another public URL, and you can then set up jobs to encode that video file to multiple formats using their web interface or via API calls. Zencoder will fetch the video files, do the encoding, and then transfer the new videos back to your servers. The service is not free, but it does produce excellent results and can save you a lot of time if you have a lot of content to encode.[4]

If you just want to experiment with these formats on your own, Miro Video Converter[5] is another nice option. It has presets for converting your video files to multiple outputs, and it's open source.

---

2. http://www.ffmpeg.org/
3. http://www.zencoder.com/
4. In the interest of full disclosure, I know a couple of developers at Zencoder, but I would still recommend the service if I didn't.
5. http://mirovideoconverter.com/

Resources

A4.1 Resources on the Web

Apple—HTML5 . . . . http://www.apple.com/html5/
Apple's page on HTML5 and web standards as supported by its Safari 5 web browser.

CSS3.Info http://www.css3.info/
Lots of background information and examples related to the various modules that make up CSS3.

Font Squirrel . . . . http://www.fontsquirrel.com
Provides royalty-free fonts in various formats suitable for distribution on the Web.

HTML5 . . . . http://www.w3.org/TR/html5/
The actual HTML5 specification at the W3C.

HTML5—Mozilla Developer Center . . . .
. . . . https://developer.mozilla.org/en/html/html5
Mozilla Developer Center's page on HTML5.

Implementing Web Socket Servers with Node.js . . . .
. . http://www.web2media.net/laktek/2010/05/04/implementing-web-socket-servers-with-node-js/
How to write Web Sockets servers with Node.js.

Microsoft IE9 Test-Drive . . . . http://ie.microsoft.com/testdrive/
Demonstrations of HTML5 (and related) features in Internet Explorer 9.

Ruby and WebSockets—TCP for the Browser . . . .
. . . . http://www.igvita.com/2009/12/22/ruby-websockets-tcp-for-the-browser/
Information on em-websocket, a Ruby library for building Web Sockets servers.

Setting Up a Flash Policy File . . . .
. . . . http://www.lightsphere.com/dev/articles/flash_socket_policy.html
Contains a detailed description of Flash Socket Policy files.

Typekit . . . . http://www.typekit.com
Service that lets you use licensed fonts on your website using a simple Java-Script API.

Unit Interactive: "Better CSS Font Stacks" . . . .
. . . . http://unitinteractive.com/blog/2008/06/26/better-css-font-stacks/
Discussion of font stacks, with some excellent examples.

Video for Everybody! . . . . http://camendesign.com/code/video_for_everybody
Information on HTML5 video, with code to play video on all browsers.

Video.js . . . . http://videojs.com
JavaScript library to aid in playing HTML5 videos.

When Can I Use... . . . . http://caniuse.com/
Browser compatibility tables for HTML5, CSS3, and related technologies.

Bibliography

[HT00]   Andrew Hunt and David Thomas. *The Pragmatic Programmer: From Journey-man to Master*. Addison-Wesley, Reading, MA, 2000.

[Hog09]   Brian P. Hogan. *Web Design For Developers*. The Pragmatic Bookshelf, Raleigh, NC and Dallas, TX, 2009.

[Zel09]   Jeffrey Zeldman. *Designing With Web Standards*. New Riders Press, Upper Saddle River, NJ, 2009.

Index

Go Beyond with Rails and NoSQL

There's so much new to learn with Rails 3 and the latest crop of NoSQL databases. These titles will get you up to speed on the latest.

Thousands of developers have used the first edition of *Rails Recipes* to solve the hard problems. Now, five years later, it's time for the Rails 3.1 edition of this trusted collection of solutions, completely revised by Rails master Chad Fowler.

Chad Fowler
(350 pages) ISBN: 9781934356777. $35
http://pragprog.com/titles/rr2

Data is getting bigger and more complex by the day, and so are your choices in handling it. From traditional RDBMS to newer NoSQL approaches, *Seven Databases in Seven Weeks* takes you on a tour of some of the hottest open source databases today. In the tradition of Bruce A. Tate's *Seven Languages in Seven Weeks*, this book goes beyond your basic tutorial to explore the essential concepts at the core of each technology.

Eric Redmond and Jim Wilson
(330 pages) ISBN: 9781934356920. $35
http://pragprog.com/titles/rwdata

Welcome to the New Web

You need a better JavaScript and more expressive CSS and HTML today. Start here.

CoffeeScript is JavaScript done right. It provides all of JavaScript's functionality wrapped in a cleaner, more succinct syntax. In the first book on this exciting new language, CoffeeScript guru Trevor Burnham shows you how to hold onto all the power and flexibility of JavaScript while writing clearer, cleaner, and safer code.

Trevor Burnham
(136 pages) ISBN: 9781934356784. $29
http://pragprog.com/titles/tbcoffee

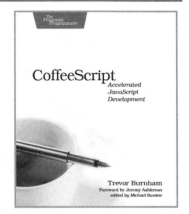

CSS is fundamental to the web, but it's a basic language and lacks many features. Sass is just like CSS, but with a whole lot of extra power so you can get more done, more quickly. Build better web pages today with *Pragmatic Guide to Sass*. These concise, easy-to-digest tips and techniques are the shortcuts experienced CSS developers need to start developing in Sass today.

Hampton Catlin and Michael Lintorn Catlin
(100 pages) ISBN: 9781934356845. $25
http://pragprog.com/titles/pg_sass

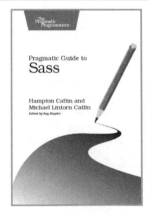

Pragmatic Guide Series

Get started quickly, with a minimum of fuss and hand-holding. The Pragmatic Guide Series features convenient, task-oriented two-page spreads. You'll find what you need fast, and get on with your work.

Need to learn how to wrap your head around Git, but don't need a lot of hand holding? Grab this book if you're new to Git, not to the world of programming. Git tasks displayed on two-page spreads provide all the context you need, without the extra fluff.

NEW: Part of the new *Pragmatic Guide* series

Travis Swicegood
(168 pages) ISBN: 9781934356722. $25
http://pragprog.com/titles/pg_git

JavaScript is everywhere. It's a key component of today's Web—a powerful, dynamic language with a rich ecosystem of professional-grade development tools, infrastructures, frameworks, and toolkits. This book will get you up to speed quickly and painlessly with the 35 key JavaScript tasks you need to know.

NEW: Part of the new *Pragmatic Guide* series

Christophe Porteneuve
(150 pages) ISBN: 9781934356678. $25
http://pragprog.com/titles/pg_js

Testing is only the beginning

Start with Test Driven Development, Domain Driven Design, and Acceptance Test Driven Planning in Ruby. Then add Shoulda, Cucumber, Factory Girl, and Rcov for the ultimate in Ruby and Rails development.

Behaviour-Driven Development (BDD) gives you the best of Test Driven Development, Domain Driven Design, and Acceptance Test Driven Planning techniques, so you can create better software with self-documenting, executable tests that bring users and developers together with a common language.

Get the most out of BDD in Ruby with *The RSpec Book*, written by the lead developer of RSpec, David Chelimsky.

David Chelimsky, Dave Astels, Zach Dennis, Aslak Hellesøy, Bryan Helmkamp, Dan North
(448 pages) ISBN: 9781934356371. $38.95
http://pragprog.com/titles/achbd

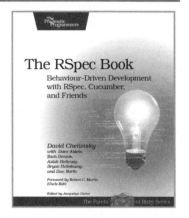

Rails Test Prescriptions is a comprehensive guide to testing Rails applications, covering Test-Driven Development from both a theoretical perspective (why to test) and from a practical perspective (how to test effectively). It covers the core Rails testing tools and procedures for Rails 2 and Rails 3, and introduces popular add-ons, including RSpec, Shoulda, Cucumber, Factory Girl, and Rcov.

Noel Rappin
(368 pages) ISBN: 9781934356647. $34.95
http://pragprog.com/titles/nrtest

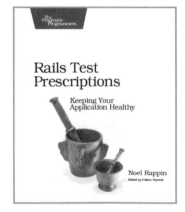

Advanced Ruby and Rails

What used to be the realm of experts is fast becoming the stuff of day-to-day development. Jump to the head of the class in Ruby and Rails.

Rails 3 is a huge step forward. You can now easily extend the framework, change its behavior, and replace whole components to bend it to your will, all without messy hacks. This pioneering book is the first resource that deep dives into the new Rails 3 APIs and shows you how to use them to write better web applications and make your day-to-day work with Rails more productive.

José Valim
(180 pages) ISBN: 9781934356739. $33
http://pragprog.com/titles/jvrails

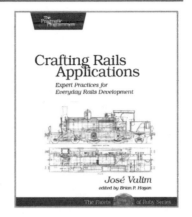

As a Ruby programmer, you already know how much fun it is. Now see how to unleash its power, digging under the surface and exploring the language's most advanced features: a collection of techniques and tricks known as *metaprogramming*. Once the domain of expert Rubyists, metaprogramming is now accessible to programmers of all levels—from beginner to expert. *Metaprogramming Ruby* explains metaprogramming concepts in a down-to-earth style and arms you with a practical toolbox that will help you write great Ruby code.

Paolo Perrotta
(240 pages) ISBN: 9781934356470. $32.95
http://pragprog.com/titles/ppmetr

Be Agile

Don't just "do" agile; you want to *be* agile. We'll show you how.

The best agile book isn't a book: *Agile in a Flash* is a unique deck of index cards that fit neatly in your pocket. You can tape them to the wall. Spread them out on your project table. Get stains on them over lunch. These cards are meant to be used, not just read.

Jeff Langr and Tim Ottinger
(110 pages) ISBN: 9781934356715. $15
http://pragprog.com/titles/olag

Here are three simple truths about software development:

1. You can't gather all the requirements up front. 2. The requirements you do gather will change. 3. There is always more to do than time and money will allow.

Those are the facts of life. But you can deal with those facts (and more) by becoming a fierce software-delivery professional, capable of dispatching the most dire of software projects and the toughest delivery schedules with ease and grace.

Jonathan Rasmusson
(280 pages) ISBN: 9781934356586. $34.95
http://pragprog.com/titles/jtrap